THE ART OF
DANISH LIVING

How to Find Happiness
In and Out of Work

MEIK WIKING

PENGUIN LIFE

UK | USA | Canada | Ireland | Australia
India | New Zealand | South Africa

Penguin Life is part of the Penguin Random House group of companies
whose addresses can be found at global.penguinrandomhouse.com.

Penguin
Random House
UK

First published 2024
001

Lyrics from ' Freedom!' written and performed by George Michael

Quotation from the 2007 *Mad Men* episode 'Smoke Gets in Your Eyes', written by Matthew Weiner

Colour origination by Altaimage, London
Printed and bound in Italy by Printer Trento

The authorized representative in the EEA is Penguin Random House Ireland,
Morrison Chambers, 32 Nassau Street, Dublin DO2 YH68

A CIP catalogue record for this book is available from the British Library

ISBN: 978-0-241-63827-9

MIX
Paper | Supporting
responsible forestry
FSC® C018179
FSC
www.fsc.org

Contents

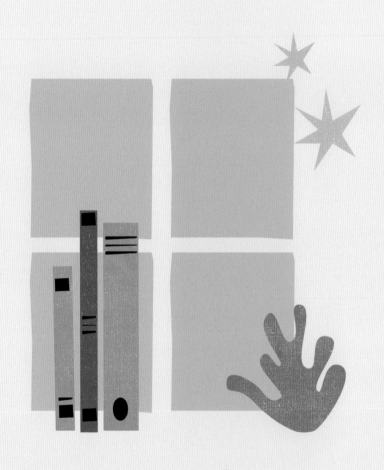

CHAPTER

1

WORK JOY

I still remember my first day working at the Royal Danish Ministry of Foreign Affairs. I had been to an interview with the deputy head of the department for Africa and visited the building just once before. I was looking forward to starting work.

Shortly after arriving, I met my interviewer again. She welcomed me and introduced me to the head of the office.

'So, you are the new guy,' he said. 'What languages do you speak?'

'English, Danish and Sønderjysk,' I replied. Sønderjysk is the dialect of Danish that is spoken in the part of Denmark where I grew up, close to the German border. It is very difficult to understand even for other Danes so I would argue it could be called a separate language. I thought that was very funny. But my new boss did not.

'You don't speak French?' he replied. 'Then what are you doing here?' Before I could muster a single '*Pardon?*' he was on his way, with the deputy office manager by his side and my self-esteem crushed under his shoes.

He may have had a point. Benin, Burkina Faso, Congo and many other countries in Africa have French as the official language, so I could see the sense in hiring people who speak French. I didn't understand why he wanted to rub that in my face on my very first day though.

However, I soon learned that I was not the only one he was displeased with. 'You are an idiot!' he once yelled at another student assistant, and I heard him ask a third whether she had brain malaria. For a person who should excel in diplomacy, he had very little diplomatic sense.

During that time I was still studying, and my professor in economics was simply brilliant. There were three different professors teaching the same course and we students could go to any of the classes. In the two other classes there were five or six students attending. In Anders' class there were 200 students. He was excellent at communicating complex issues in a manner that was easy to understand – and furthermore he was a really nice and jolly fellow.

After my final economics exam, Anders asked if I would be interested in starting as his intern at a think tank called Monday Morning, focusing on welfare and sustainability. I said yes at once. The following week, I went into my boss's office at the department for Africa and gave my notice. He was not happy that they now had to train someone new for my position. I had been there for ten months. In the movie version, I would have given my notice in French. The sky was a special kind of blue as I cycled home that afternoon.

The point of the story is: there are many things in life that are wonderful – going on holiday, having fun with your friends, eating a delicious dinner. But have you ever quit a job that was bad for your mental health?

If not, then hopefully you will find some inspiration in this book. But we should aim higher than just quitting crappy jobs. This book is about raising the bar for happiness at work. It is about how we can shape and create work and workplaces that allow us to thrive.

More than a decade ago, I founded the Happiness Research Institute, and I have worked there ever since. I know it sounds like a magical place and people imagine our office to be packed with unicorns and fudge, and that my schedule for Monday is: Ice cream, Ice cream, Ice cream – Lunch – Puppies, Puppies, Puppies. That is unfortunately not the case. We look less at unicorns and puppies, and more at randomized controlled trials and peer-reviewed papers.

But my superpower of being a naive Danish happiness researcher means that I believe work can and should be a source of happiness. That is also the premise and promise of this book: that work can be fun and fulfilling – if we design it right.

In this book, we will look at what drives happiness at work. We will consider which factors have a positive impact on happiness. We will learn about concrete cases, work policies and experiments that have increased wellbeing at work, and we will take a closer look at Danish workplaces – and a unique and quirky Danish word: *arbejdsglæde*.

Arbejdsglæde

Allow me to provide a short guide to pronouncing the word 'arbejdsglæde': First, take a huge bite of an apple, get it stuck mid-throat and then say 'ahh-bites-gle-the'.

'Arbejde' means 'work' and 'glæde' means 'joy'. Combine the two words and hey presto, you like what you do and you feel happy about going to work. Similarly, the Danish word arbejdslyst means 'a desire to work' or 'to feel like working', and you can wish your Danish colleagues 'God arbejdslyst!', meaning that you hope people will enjoy the work they are to do and that they will feel like doing it.

'Arbejdsglæde' exists in Nordic languages – like Danish, Swedish, Norwegian and Icelandic – but as far as I can tell, there is no word for it in any other language in the world. The closest I could detect is the Estonian word 'tööröõm', which I understand means 'work fun', or finding simple joys in everyday tasks.

However, it is easy to find words that describe the other end of the spectrum. For instance, in Japanese there is the word 'karoshi', which literally means 'death from overwork'. Grinding, burning out, hitting the wall may be less dramatic terms – but perhaps they are just earlier stops along the same track.

Arbejdsglæde isn't just a nice idea either – it seems to shine through in the data, as Danes consistently report some of the highest levels of happiness at work in the world. According to Eurostat, almost two out of three Danes report a high level of job satisfaction. To put that into perspective, only about a third of German or Finnish employees feel the same way. But perhaps even more telling is the fact that 58 per cent of Danes say they would continue to work even if they no longer needed to for financial reasons – even, for instance, if they won the equivalent of £10 million in the lottery, according to one study by YouGov.

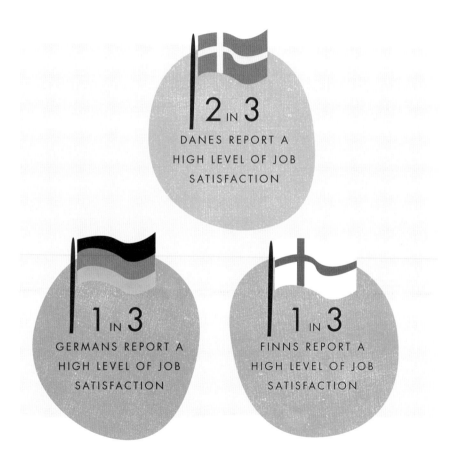

2 IN 3
DANES REPORT A
HIGH LEVEL OF JOB
SATISFACTION

1 IN 3
GERMANS REPORT A
HIGH LEVEL OF JOB
SATISFACTION

1 IN 3
FINNS REPORT A
HIGH LEVEL OF JOB
SATISFACTION

It is because of findings like these, along with its ranking as one of the happiest countries on earth in the UN's annual *World Happiness Report*, that Denmark is sometimes thought of as a utopia. In *The Little Book of Lykke* I wanted to poke fun at this idea and wrote:

> *Around the city free boxes of LEGO are handed out as part of a national strategy to stimulate creativity, innovation and design. Everything runs smoothly here. Well, almost. Four years ago, one train did arrive five minutes late. The passengers each got a letter of apology from the prime minister and a designer chair of their choice as compensation.*

After the book was published, I received an email from a journalist from one of the biggest newspapers in the US, who asked whether my anecdote about the letters was true or just a joke.

'It was a joke,' I wrote back. 'Our trains are never late.'

The point is, though, that Denmark cannot live up to the reputation it has. No country can really be a utopia. Of course there are people in Denmark who are unhappy, be that at home or at work, or both. A lot of the rankings are based on averages, and inevitably there are people above and below the average. When we undertake studies at the Happiness Research Institute, we cover both groups, as well as those in the middle of the spectrum. We do want to know how happy people are – but perhaps even more important is to understand why. Why do some people report 10 out of 10 when it comes to their satisfaction with life or with work, while others report 1 on the same scale – and what can we learn from this? What are the drivers and barriers for happiness at work?

We have conducted studies in Denmark and internationally, looking at which factors explain why some people are happier with their jobs than others.

We define being happy at work as looking forward to work tomorrow, having enjoyed work yesterday, and thinking that your workplace is a great place to work. But rather than analysing who is happiest, we want to know what the determining factors are: is it the salary level, a person's relationship with their boss or a sense of achievement that explains differences in our happiness levels?

At the Happiness Research Institute, we have worked with smaller companies, with just a couple of hundred employees, as well as global organizations, with several hundred thousand employees. In this book, I will share insights from those studies, to show how anyone can adjust their perspectives, habits and behaviours to feel happier both at work and in their life outside of it.

When we run happiness surveys in companies and organizations, we make sure that the employees remain anonymous but that at the same time we can track individual participants over time. So, while we don't know that it is Karen in accounting who last month reported 6 on a scale from 0 to 10 when it came to happiness at work and now reports 8, we do know that it is the same respondent. That is important, because it is the development – the ups and downs – that we are interested in understanding. If 10 per cent of employees experienced an increase in wellbeing at work after a new flexibility policy was introduced, for instance, that is clearly something that works.

In comparison, the yoga sessions, massages, nap pods, laundry services and the free smoothies that we hear about in Silicon Valley don't seem to move the dial. Such perks may impact whether you say that your workplace overall is a good place to work, but they will not have an impact on whether you feel happy at work, whether you enjoyed yesterday or look forward to tomorrow. And *that* is our ambition. To reveal and understand what actually makes us happy at work, how we can all learn to reduce stress, increase positivity and work like the happiest people on earth. But first, let's take a closer look at how work and happiness are connected.

The Complexity of Work

If work and happiness had to select their relationship status on Facebook, they would probably go for 'It's complicated'.

Although work is the source of a lot of stress, pressure and anxiety for many, it is obvious that losing a job has a negative impact on a person's wellbeing. We lose a source of income, but we may also lose many of the social relationships we had cultivated at work, a part of our identity and a sense of purpose.

When researchers follow large groups of people over time to understand how changes in their lives impact their wellbeing, we see that losing your job takes a big toll on happiness. So does going through a divorce and getting sick. This is all perhaps unsurprising, but what is less obvious is that we actually recover rather quickly from a lot of setbacks in life. We often bounce back from divorce and illness and return to previous happiness levels relatively quickly – but that isn't the case with unemployment. The emotional impact of unemployment can still be as bad three years after the fact, and it often gets worse as time passes.

If we look at data from the British Household Panel, we can see that people who experience unemployment will report a drop in life satisfaction of 1 point on a 10-point scale one year after losing their job. Four years later – if they are still unemployed – they will likely drop an additional 0.5 points. For a comparison, let me tell you that the same survey shows that people who get married experience on average an increase in life satisfaction of 0.65 points the year they get married, compared to four years before their marriage. In short, you would need the emotional boost of two weddings to counter the negative impact of one year of unemployment.

In the studies I have seen, involuntarily unemployed people are always less happy. No matter whether we think of happiness as an overall satisfaction with life, a sense of purpose and meaning or the experiencing of positive emotions like joy and excitement on a day-to-day basis – and in happiness research we usually include all these elements – unemployed people consistently score lower than their employed counterparts.

On average, people who are employed experience a satisfaction that is 0.6 points higher (on a scale from 0 to 10) than those who are unemployed. This difference may not sound like a lot, but globally speaking the average satisfaction with life is roughly around 5 – so it means being about 10 per cent happier. And if we look at what kind of emotions we experience on a day-to-day basis, unemployed people feel around 30 per cent more negative emotions compared to people who are employed.

The studies we have conducted at the Happiness Research Institute among the general population have found that happiness at work and a person's overall happiness are connected. If you are happy at work, you are more likely to be happy with life overall. It makes sense – we spend so many hours at work and if those hours are packed with positive emotions, a strong sense of purpose, pride in what we have achieved and lots of awesome people who get you and support you, then naturally, your alarm clock will sound less horrible at 7 a.m. on a rainy Monday. We can also see in the data that when your happiness at work increases by 1 point your overall happiness will likely also increase (by 0.5 points). So, when your happiness at work increases, so does your general happiness. Yay! Double-win.

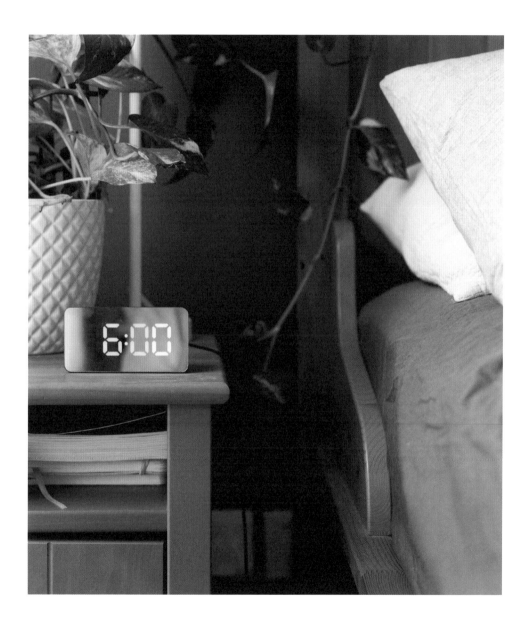

To sum up: our jobs are vital to our wellbeing. Or, as the *World Happiness Report* from 2017 put it, 'The notion that employment matters greatly for the wellbeing of individuals is one of the most robust results to have come out of the economic study of human happiness.'

However, when you look at how people are feeling when they are at work, the results are not splendid. Not having a job is bad for happiness – and a cause of worry, stress and lack of purpose and structure. But having a job is sometimes also bad for happiness – and a cause of worry and stress.

One of the researchers who has documented this is Daniel Kahneman, the psychologist who received the 2002 Nobel Prize in Economics. At the turn of the twenty-first century, he and his team looked at working women in Texas, using a then-pioneering approach called the Day Reconstruction Method. They followed the moment-to-moment experiences and emotions that made up an ordinary day for nearly a thousand different individuals. The 909 women in the study kept a diary of everything they did during the day, from washing laundry and watching television to having sex and commuting to work.

The following day, the women would consult their notes and rate each activity in terms of how it had made them feel; for instance, they might have put annoyed, worried, depressed, warm or happy. The net effect was then calculated by the researchers. Was the activity something that mostly brought out good or bad emotions, and to what degree? The top five activities – the ones that made the good times roll – were intimate relations (or to put it in even more academic terms: bow-chicka-wow-wow), socializing after work, relaxing, having dinner and having lunch. So, essentially, activities that are good for our survival as a species make us feel good. At the bottom of the list, Kahneman and his team found housework, childcare, the evening commute, work and – worst of all – the morning commute.

But, you might say, maybe people misremembered how they felt one day later. Maybe if we had asked them while they were working how they felt, we would have seen different results.

This is a good point, and to shed some light on it, let me tell you about the Mappiness Project, which was led by the British economics lecturer George McKerron. In 2010, the Mappiness Project began a research mission at the London School of Economics, where study participants were randomly 'pinged' several times a day via their smartphones and asked how happy they were right then and there. In the same moment, the participants were also asked where they were and what they were doing right then. They had forty different activity options to choose from, including working, and could also note whether they were alone, and if they weren't, who they were with.

The researchers were able to collect more than a million observations from tens of thousands of individuals in the UK. They found that paid work was ranked lower than any of the other thirty-nine activities people engage in (not all shown in the graph), except for 'being sick in bed'. Working had one of the worst impacts on happiness.

TOP 5 ACTIVITIES

How Do Different Activities Impact Happiness?

Impact on happiness of different activities

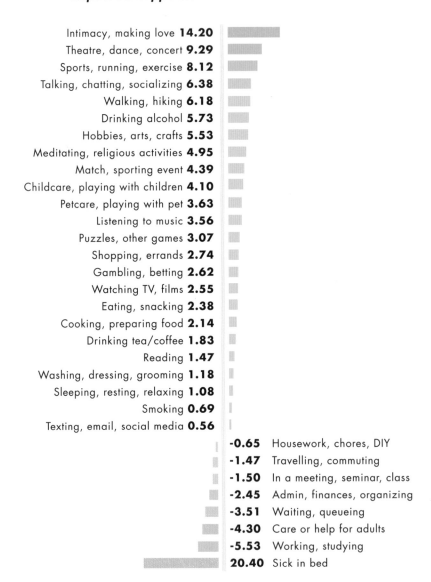

Intimacy, making love **14.20**

Theatre, dance, concert **9.29**

Sports, running, exercise **8.12**

Talking, chatting, socializing **6.38**

Walking, hiking **6.18**

Drinking alcohol **5.73**

Hobbies, arts, crafts **5.53**

Meditating, religious activities **4.95**

Match, sporting event **4.39**

Childcare, playing with children **4.10**

Petcare, playing with pet **3.63**

Listening to music **3.56**

Puzzles, other games **3.07**

Shopping, errands **2.74**

Gambling, betting **2.62**

Watching TV, films **2.55**

Eating, snacking **2.38**

Cooking, preparing food **2.14**

Drinking tea/coffee **1.83**

Reading **1.47**

Washing, dressing, grooming **1.18**

Sleeping, resting, relaxing **1.08**

Smoking **0.69**

Texting, email, social media **0.56**

-0.65 Housework, chores, DIY

-1.47 Travelling, commuting

-1.50 In a meeting, seminar, class

-2.45 Admin, finances, organizing

-3.51 Waiting, queueing

-4.30 Care or help for adults

-5.53 Working, studying

20.40 Sick in bed

Well, you might say, those two studies' results are only from Texas and the UK. Things might be different across the globe. Unfortunately not. According to Gallup, only 20 per cent of all people globally are thriving at work, 62 per cent have 'quietly quit' or feel disengaged. 'Quiet quitting' refers to doing the bare minimum requirements of one's job and putting in no more time or effort than absolutely necessary. And 18 per cent have 'loudly quit' or are actively disengaged.

Not only do we often feel less happy at work than we do elsewhere but our work can sometimes literally make us sick. In the US, the Centers for Disease Control found that seven out of ten people had at least one symptom of workplace stress such as regular headaches or feeling consistently anxious or overwhelmed. When I type 'work is' into Google, one of the most popular suggestions to finish that sentence is 'da poop' – and maybe that sums it up for a lot of people. More concerningly, though, 'making me sick' and 'giving me anxiety' are also top results.

So, what do we do about that? Well, a good first step is picking up this book. Well done you – yes, I am heavily biased – but still, well done you! Because it means that you believe there is something we can do. Yes, 'we'. Happiness at work is a shared responsibility. It is not just up to you, or your boss or the organization you work for – we all have the responsibility to increase happiness at work. In the chapters to come, we will explore how to achieve that. I will also give you tips on how to make your manager see the value in focusing on and increasing wellbeing among employees. In fact, here is a suggested script for the next time you are chatting with your boss.

You: 'So did you see the cool study conducted by researchers at the University of Oxford's Saïd Business School and Erasmus University Rotterdam examining the link between productivity and happiness?'

Boss (*obviously lying*): 'Sure, but I would love to hear your take on it.'

You: 'Well, as you know, De Neve, Ward and Bellet worked with British Telecom and tracked the happiness levels of their sales staff. They followed 1,800 people in six different locations on a weekly basis for six months. Using a simple email survey, the employees were asked to rate their current state of happiness at a given time from very sad to very happy.'

Boss: 'Mmhhm, yes. Very happy.'

You: 'Right, and they also tracked productivity.'

Boss: 'Yes, productivity. Very important. Very, very important.'

You: 'It is, boss. So, the researchers collected data on absence, sick days, breaks, calls per hour and how many of the calls were converted to sales.'

Boss: 'Yes, sales. The foundation of business. Must increase sales.'

You: 'What they found was that when employees are happier they are more productive – they make more calls per hour worked – and perhaps most importantly, they converted more of their calls into sales. Do you know how much more productive they are?'

Boss: 'Yes.'

Awkward pause

You (*breaking the silence*): 'Thirteen per cent.'

Boss: 'Per cent, yes.'

You: 'And the researchers say that while the relationship between wellbeing and work has often been debated, this is the first time we have evidence of the causality. Happier workers are more productive. They found that the happier workers are not working more hours than their less happy co-workers – they are just more productive when they work.'

Boss: 'I love sales. I mean science. I love science.'

You: 'That's great, boss.'

You could have also told your manager that this study found happier employees have fewer sick days and are more loyal to the company, which reduces expensive staff turnover, and a whole range of other side benefits that managers should be interested in. Increasing happiness at work is the right thing to do – but it also makes good business sense.

In addition, the pandemic made us reconsider work. How, when and why. And companies have increasingly recognized their role and their responsibility for the mental health of their employees.

The growing evidence that happier employees are good for the bottom line is the reason why companies like Google, Airbnb, Amazon and SAP have all created a Chief Happiness Officer role within their executive ranks.

We will revisit the Chief Happiness Officer concept later in the book – but first, allow me to assign you some happy homework, aka happywork, to help you apply the learnings from this chapter to your own life.

HAPPYWORK

❑ Think like an archaeologist looking back through time – which jobs have you had in the past and how would you rate them in terms of happiness at work from 0 to 5? Which elements were good and bad about your previous jobs?

❑ Start mapping which moments and days provide you with *arbejdsglæde* currently – what happens on those days when you think on your way home, 'That was a great day at work'?

❑ Embrace the complexity of happiness at work. Yes, work can be tough and stressful at times – but stress at work should not be a permanent state. If things aren't changing for the better at work, it might be better to change your job.

❑ Consider which elements of your job and happiness at work you have control over and which you don't. You might not be able to change a toxic boss, but perhaps you can influence the number of days you are in the office, or who you sit with.

❑ Talk with your co-workers and your manager about the research which shows that happier workers are more productive and see what they think. Try to get to know what drives happiness at work for them.

❑ Embrace that you are also responsible for your happiness at work. Yes, your organization *and* your manager both should care and can move the needle – but so can you.

CHAPTER

2

FINDING PURPOSE

'So, what do you do?'

. . . is perhaps one of the most frequently asked questions whenever we meet someone new at a dinner party, besides 'So, how do you know Frank and Jenny?' and 'Could you pass me the mashed potatoes, please?'

The answer to this question helps people put us in preconceived boxes and prompts certain conversation paths. I will experience two different levels of follow-up questions depending on whether I answer that I work in happiness research or – equally true – in statistics.

Imagine animals engaging in the same form of conversation. 'So, basically, I work in supply-chain management in the food industry, bananas mostly.'

A lot of us find identity in and through our work – though that can change throughout our lives. Less of my identity was tied up in my work when I was making Danish pastries on the nightshift at the local bakery when I was twenty-two, compared with being a writer and happiness researcher at the age of forty-two.

Nevertheless, perhaps a more interesting question to pose when you meet someone new could be not what do you do but *why* do you do it. Because the answer to that question is a good indicator of your happiness at work. Yes, we work to make ends meet financially – but that is not necessarily everything.

We ran a survey at the Happiness Research Institute in Denmark to explore the drivers that make some people happier with their jobs than others. We looked at the importance of colleagues, bosses, feeling that you are good at your job, achieving results, finding a balance between work and life, and salary levels. We ran the survey over several years – and we also looked at Norway one year (it turns out Norwegians are very much like Danes but with a nicer-sounding language and a more beautiful landscape). But in the end we found the same result, year after year. There was one factor that always stood out as the most important in terms of explaining why some people were happier with their work than others: having a sense of purpose.

In this research, we used a wide definition of purpose – looking at whether people felt they were making the world a better place as well as whether they thought their function in the greater organization made sense and felt meaningful or they thought they were just moving papers around. What we found was that people working in smaller organizations were more likely to feel meaningful *within* their company. People in both small and large organizations felt they were making the world a better place. And both the 'large meaning' (making the world a better place) and the 'small meaning' (having a role of importance within the organization) matter for our sense of purpose – and for our happiness at work. We have a much easier time getting up in the morning – and find our jobs much more enjoyable – if we are fuelled with the fire of *why* we do what we do. Later in this chapter we will explore the idea of job crafting, which can help you find more meaning in your current job and also understand which alternative careers might feel more meaningful.

Or to put it in the words of Antoine de Saint-Exupéry, the author of *The Little Prince*, 'If you want to build a ship, don't drum up people to collect wood and don't assign them tasks and work, but rather teach them to long for the endless immensity of the sea.'

To enjoy the process, we need to understand that instead of pursuing happiness –

thinking that happiness is something we can reach at a certain destination if we run fast enough – we need to value the happiness of pursuit.

People on a quest for something they find meaningful, whether that is building a ship or a company or a happiness museum, tend to be happier. The process of building a happiness museum meant that I got to look for ancient coins featuring the goddess Felicitas in Rome, buy 8.2 kilograms of sweets (the amount the average Dane consumes in a year) and work with my dad, who managed the renovation of the location, all in the name of hygge. There was also the brilliant but awkward moment when I had to ask my colleague Alejandro whether his parents could bring a replica of a Pompeiian relief with the inscription 'Hic habitas felicitas' ('Here lives happiness') to Copenhagen when they visited – the inscription was found over a phallus, hence the slightly awkward conversation.

Speaking of the Happiness Museum in Copenhagen, my favourite part of it is the room where we ask the guests to write down on a Post-it what makes them happy. The walls are now covered with thousands of yellow stickers. Pizza night, a warm hug from my friend Sophie, dogs, and Mum's apple crumble are just some of the answers. All great – and all valid if we look at the data from happiness research. However, I think my all-time favourite is the Post-it where someone wrote that happiness is 'a good-quality lawnmower and a big lawn to mow'. It is easy to see what part of the lawn you have mowed and where you have not been yet. We like to see our progress. It is why the first coat of paint is more fun to do than the second coat. It is why we write things down on our to-do list that we have already done so that we can cross them out – please tell me that I am not the only one who does that.

Neither the Post-its nor the study we did around meaning would come as a surprise to Dan Ariely, who is a professor of psychology and behavioural economics at Duke University.

'Would you like to build this LEGO Bionicle figurine for three dollars?' he asked people, as part of an experiment.

Once the participant had assembled one figurine, the researcher would take the figurine and put it under the desk, and the participant was asked if they would assemble another figurine for 30 cents less. The third would earn them $2.40, the fourth $2.10 and so on. This was the set-up for half of the participants. The other half were also asked to assemble figurines and were also offered $3 for the first, $2.70 for the second and so on. The only difference between the two groups was that once the participants from the second group had assembled their first figurine and started working on the second, the researcher would start to tear the first figurine apart (instead of putting it under the table like he or she did with the first group). So only two sets of LEGO were in play. One was being assembled as the other was being disassembled.

This was considered the 'Sisyphus scenario' of the experiment, named after the guy in ancient Greek myth who was doomed to push a rock up a hill for all eternity; each time he got to the top, the rock would roll back down the hill and Sisyphus had to start over again. In the second group, who had to watch their just-finished work being torn apart in front of them, people would assemble on average seven figurines before declining to assemble the next one for 90 cents. But in the first group, people were far from done at figurine number seven. In fact, on average they finished eleven figurines – almost 60 per cent more. Not only that, the last figurine was assembled just for the fun of it, as it paid 0 cents.

This might be a very simple experiment – but it illustrates such an important point. If something as straightforward as whether the figurine we just built is being kept or torn apart makes us work 60 per cent more and think that it is so much fun that we are willing to build one for free, how does the real-life experience of meaningful work play out – and perhaps more importantly, what can we do to experience an increase in the sense of meaning in our work?

In some organizations, of course, it is easy to spot the greater good that you are working towards. Workers in an NGO trying to end world hunger can easily understand and communicate their purpose, while workers in a company selling rubber toys for dogs may struggle more. Sticks are a tough competitor! But there are other ways that you can choose to donate money or time to good causes. Some companies allow employees to do community work one day a year. We decided to donate one month's profits from the Happiness Museum to the Red Cross in Ukraine in March 2022. If you are a manager, consider the following: how can we make the long-term goal of the organization clearer? How do we show our employees that their work is important for our overall goal? Do we have the financial strength to donate part of our profits to charity? Or can we better show our employees all the good that comes from their efforts?

Hey, Boss, Where Are All These Springs Going?

Some tasks can seem pointless, but an understanding of how they fit into the bigger picture – and how our collective work has a positive impact on the world – may add meaning and make work more enjoyable. I visited a spring-making company many years ago, and the way they achieved this was to gather their employees once a year to show them a film of where the springs they had been making had gone. The springs were used in everything from fire alarms to beds and so they helped to save people from fires and reduced bedsores for hospital patients, among other things. In this way, the company made it clear what their long-term goal was and how everyone's work would impact people's lives.

If your boss can't see the point of the above, they might be interested to know that people who feel they make the world a better place through their work are often willing to work for less money. One study, 'What Price the Moral High Ground?' by Robert Frank at Cornell University, examined the employment preferences of a sample of seniors graduating from Cornell. They were faced with two similar jobs, for instance copywriter, but for two different organizations, the American Cancer Association and Camel Cigarettes – which one would you choose if they were paying the same salary?

In the study, 88.2 per cent of the graduates chose the former. And what would it take in terms of more money per year to make you switch from the more meaningful workplace to Camel? The average premium was US$24,333 – and mind you, this study took place in 1996, so that's $46,397 in today's money. So yes, the moral high ground does come with a price tag – in terms of income but perhaps also a bonus in terms of happiness.

Where to Find Meaning?

———————

'Well, that is great,' you might say. 'Meaning sounds wonderful, but where do I get it? I have searched all over Amazon and I can't find it anywhere – and I even have Amazon Prime.' Well, if you are currently considering changing career, or trying to decide which career to choose if you are just starting out, you could take some inspiration from a study by PayScale. PayScale is a US company that collects big data about salaries and careers from more than 50 million people with more than 10,000 unique job titles. With that data we can explore pay equity and salary levels but also people's job satisfaction and sense of meaning. Of the more than 500 different titles with sufficient data, the most meaningful role is in the clergy, where 98 per cent of people report a high level of sense of meaning. Teachers and surgeons came in second and third.

And if we examine the top thirty, we can also discover strong patterns. Jobs in the education and health (both physical and mental) sectors dominate the space. There are still some surprising entries though. For example, I wouldn't have guessed that Water and Liquid Waste Treatment Plant and System Operators would make the top thirty – but I'm happy that they do.

Top Twenty-Five Meaningful Jobs

Share of people who find a high level of sense of meaning in their job

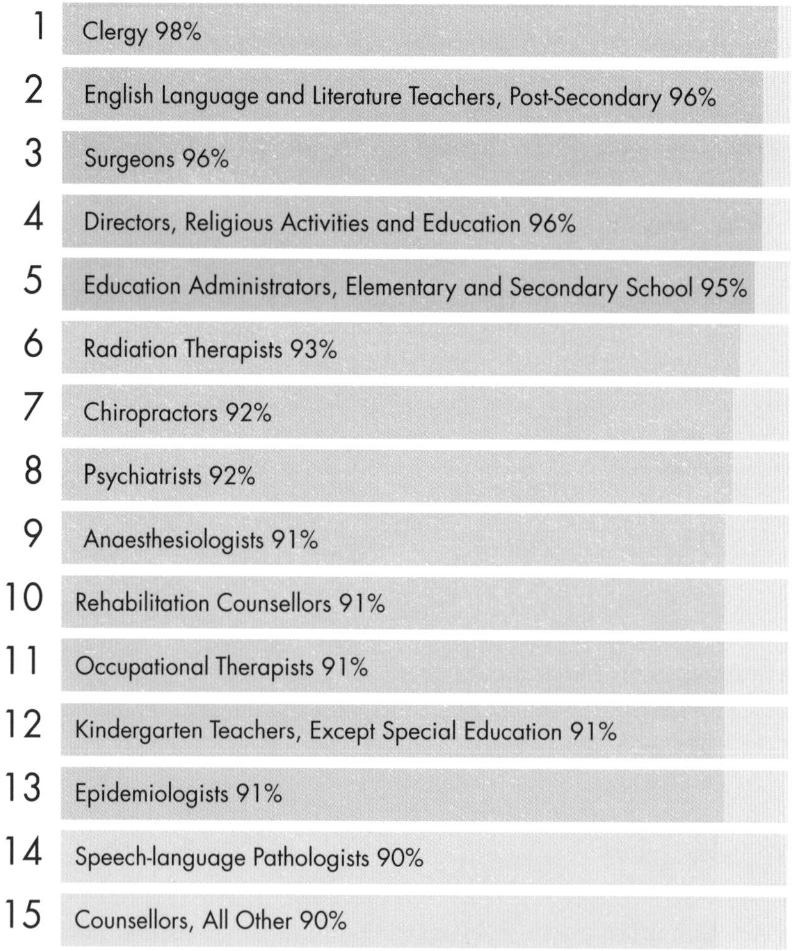

1 Clergy 98%

2 English Language and Literature Teachers, Post-Secondary 96%

3 Surgeons 96%

4 Directors, Religious Activities and Education 96%

5 Education Administrators, Elementary and Secondary School 95%

6 Radiation Therapists 93%

7 Chiropractors 92%

8 Psychiatrists 92%

9 Anaesthesiologists 91%

10 Rehabilitation Counsellors 91%

11 Occupational Therapists 91%

12 Kindergarten Teachers, Except Special Education 91%

13 Epidemiologists 91%

14 Speech-language Pathologists 90%

15 Counsellors, All Other 90%

16   Family and General Practitioners 90%

17   Medical Appliance Technicians 90%

18   First Line Supervisors/Managers of Police and Detectives 90%

19   Physical Therapists 90%

20   Education Administrators, Preschool and Childcare Centre 90%

21   Physicians and Surgeons, All Other 89%

22   Mental Health Counsellors 89%

23   Paediatricians, General 88%

24   Clinical, Counselling and School Psychologists 88%

25   Music Directors and Composers 88%

At the bottom of the 500-item list we find jobs like Parking Lot Attendant, Casino Floor Manager, and Counter and Rental Clerk with 5, 20 and 26 per cent sense of meaning respectively. Of course, this is not to say that you can't find meaning in those jobs or experience a high level of job satisfaction (if I was a car park attendant, I would listen to so many podcasts) but if you want to play the odds in finding meaningful work, the best bet seems to be one where you help people in some way.

This list may be useful if you are trying to decide which career to pursue, but what should you do if you are a car park attendant or a rental clerk, or if you are now retired? Well, perhaps one option could be to seek meaning outside paid work.

Voluntary Meaning

Around 40 per cent of Danes are involved in volunteering or charity work. They coach badminton, lead scout groups, cycle senior citizens around to visit places from their childhood, and a thousand other brilliant endeavours. They do it to make a difference, because it is fun, and to become part of a community (I am still friends with people I met in the Youth Red Cross twenty years ago).

What we know from happiness research is that people who are involved in volunteer work report higher levels of happiness than the rest of the population. This could be due to their heightened sense of purpose, the friendships they gather, or because certain types of volunteer work give you firsthand knowledge of how less fortunate people live – which may make you more grateful for all that you do have in your life. It may also have something to do with adding another layer to your identity. Remember earlier where we saw happiness levels drop significantly when people become unemployed – well, the drop is not as significant if we look at unemployed people who are involved in voluntary work. Yes, they lose their wage – but they still experience a sense of purpose, maintain relationships and an answer to the question: 'So, what do you do?'

If you are interested in voluntary work but don't know where to start, try browsing the internet for local volunteering opportunities. However, not everyone has the time to get involved in voluntary work and find additional meaning through that. So, another option could be to redesign how you think about your paid work.

Job Crafting

For about seven years, I would sell Christmas trees each December (pro-tip: December is the best month for Christmas trees). My friend Jess and I would buy trees in a rural part of Denmark and transport them to Copenhagen, where we would sell them for double the price. It was good fun – you got to stand outside, work with an axe, saw, hammer and nails, and our small shop was in a beautiful old square in central Copenhagen. Every year, the same lady would come by for a bit of Christmas magic for her grandchildren. She would bring her family to our shop and the script was that I would have hidden the perfect Christmas tree for a special loving family – and that was them.

Another nice aspect of the job was being able to adjust prices. When a slick guy would point to a tree, ask me to put it in the boot of his Mercedes and then check what the price was, it was a different price from the one I would quote to a customer who appeared to be a single parent and who inquired about pricing before choosing a smaller tree. Adding a dash of Robin Hood to Christmas made the job even more enjoyable, I found. I did not know it at the time, but I had unknowingly stumbled upon something called 'job crafting'.

A growing number of studies suggest that by looking at your job differently you can hack your way to a higher level of job satisfaction. The exercise of changing your view of work has been coined as 'job crafting' by Amy Wrzesniewski, now a professor of organizational behaviour at the Yale School of Management, and Jane

Dutton, Professor Emerita of Business Administration and Psychology at the Michigan Ross School of Business, whose research on the matter was first published more than twenty years ago. They have examined tech workers, hospital cleaners, factory workers and employees in a non-profit organization for women's rights.

Amy and her team noticed a key difference among the hospital cleaners. Some of them would see themselves solely as cleaners, while others chose to focus on other functions or even invent tasks that were not part of the job description, like making people laugh. That was the case for this one guy that Amy interviewed during her studies. As part of the janitorial staff at the hospital, his job was to clean up vomit when people were sick from chemotherapy. But his view was that the cleaning was just a segment of his job – his real job or core function was to cheer people up when they were feeling down. His job was to make people laugh. If a patient had vomited all over the floor and they were feeling ashamed about it, his go-to joke would be, 'Please keep doing that – that is how I get my paycheque. If you can get more up and aim for the floor again in the future, maybe I can get some overtime.'

We all have a list of tasks that we need to get done. But a lot of us have the opportunity to mind-hack ourselves with a redefinition of what we actually do at work, building in more of the stuff that we enjoy in our jobs.

HAPPINESS TIP: SMILE FILE

Recently, I received a message from a former intern at the Happiness Research Institute. She was congratulating me on the organization's ten-year anniversary. She also let me know that her time with us back in 2014 still influenced her – 'I still take walk-and-talks and opt for the veg option in the canteen – and I still keep in touch with Maria and Kjartan.' That made me happy – and it went right into my Smile File.

I first learned about the idea of the Smile File when Ruby Receptionist was named the number-one small company to work for in the US by *Fortune* magazine in 2015. One of the initiatives the company had implemented was to hand new employees a notebook called a Smile File, with the encouragement to write down compliments they received from co-workers, clients and managers. Whether you write these things down in a notebook or save them in a folder on your computer or phone, it is inexpensive, easy and really handy to have them to revisit on those days when things aren't going your way.

Pro tip: The Smile File is also really useful to browse through if you are preparing for a job interview or a performance review. We are often our own worst critic and tend to remember criticism far better than praise, so this is a way to make it last longer.

This is also why, if you want to give praise to a co-worker, supplier or manager (managers are people too, you know), you should put it in writing. No matter what you do, collecting all the evidence that you have had a positive impact on the world around you is an easy hack to make work feel more meaningful.

Meaning Goes Beyond
Happiness at Work

In this book we are exploring happiness at work – but as a happiness researcher, I feel obliged to underline the importance of purpose and meaning to our general happiness.

Purpose is so central to our wellbeing that when I and other happiness researchers measure happiness or the good life, we often include a specific dimension around meaning and purpose. This is not a new thing. A pioneer in my field was Aristotle, who wrote extensively about happiness, and I think the following quote still rings true today: 'Happiness is the meaning and the purpose of life, the whole aim and end of human existence.' But then again, I am biased. Happiness, to Aristotle, was a meaningful and purposeful life where we do what is right and practise justice and virtue. That is why this dimension in happiness research is often referred to as the 'eudaimonic dimension' or 'eudaimonia', which is the ancient Greek word for happiness that Aristotle used. It is typically seen as a contrast to the more traditional understanding of happiness as pleasure or hedonism.

Hedonism often gets bad PR, but I would argue that we need both elements in our lives. To me, the good life involves both a sense of purpose and a healthy dose of pleasure. Most people, however, often overlook purpose and meaning, which can lead to a lower level of satisfaction with life. It is therefore important to be aware of this dimension and take stock. How am I doing when it comes to meaning? To approach such a big and complex question, it may be useful to consider some of the prompts that go into eudaimonic wellbeing questionnaires.

For instance, how would you score – on a scale from 0 (strongly disagree) to 4 (strongly agree) – each of the statements below?

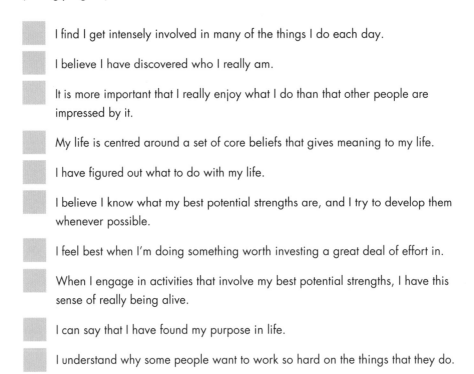

I find I get intensely involved in many of the things I do each day.

I believe I have discovered who I really am.

It is more important that I really enjoy what I do than that other people are impressed by it.

My life is centred around a set of core beliefs that gives meaning to my life.

I have figured out what to do with my life.

I believe I know what my best potential strengths are, and I try to develop them whenever possible.

I feel best when I'm doing something worth investing a great deal of effort in.

When I engage in activities that involve my best potential strengths, I have this sense of really being alive.

I can say that I have found my purpose in life.

I understand why some people want to work so hard on the things that they do.

TOTAL

If you scored 0–20, you might want to consider how to add more meaning to your work and life by revisiting this chapter.

Specialisterne

'My son was diagnosed with autism when he was three years old,' says Thorkild Sonne, who is the founder and chairman of Specialisterne.

Thorkild read about the potential future for his son. It was bleak. Autistic people were more likely to be bullied in school, drop out of education and be rejected by the labour market. In the EU, fewer than 40 per cent of people who say their disability limits their ability to work are employed. In the US, fewer than 20 per cent of people with a disability are working.

'But I wanted my son to have the same opportunities as everybody else.' At the time, Thorkild was the technical director for an IT company and he could see how the skills of autistic people might be an undervalued asset. He could see that there were countless skilled neurodivergent people who wanted to contribute to society but whose talents were being overlooked, to the detriment of employers as well as of the neurodivergent individuals.

So, in 2004 Thorkild founded Specialisterne – the name is Danish for 'The Specialists' – a company whose aim is to help neurodivergent people to thrive in the workplace by matching them with great jobs.

'We create a place for common understanding and a place where autistic people can excel in the workplace. We try to understand autistic people from a personal business profile angle. And we take the time to establish the comfort zone of the person, get to know their motivation, workability, professional and personal skills, and we take that knowledge and transfer it to managers in companies in order to set up the right work environment with the manager, the colleagues and with HR.'

Thorkild and his colleagues believe that a workforce that draws on the talents of the whole of society is better for everyone. And there is evidence to suggest that a more inclusive workforce is also good for business. 'Social responsibility makes a good business better,' says Lars Jannick Johansen. Lars is a founder and partner of Den Sociale Kapitalfond – 'the Social Capital Fund' – which seeks to create attractive returns with a positive social effect. And, full disclosure: Lars is also my former boss and we meet regularly for a friendly cup of coffee in his office by one of the canals in Copenhagen. Since 2011, the Social Capital Fund has invested in and worked with more than 150 social impact companies – delivering an annual gross return on investment of 37 per cent in its latest fund. It is a testimony to the notion that social impact does not conflict with financial results. Social inclusion means focusing on people's potential, strengthening corporate culture, workplace attraction and company branding. Or, in the words of Lars: 'Social inclusion is an indicator of quality business leadership.'

Specialisterne now operates in twelve countries and more than 10,000 jobs have been created for people with different abilities. The goal is to generate meaningful employment for one million neurodivergent people through social entrepreneurship, corporate sector engagement and a global change in mindset.

The Progress Principle

A feeling of progress is important to us all. There is a sense of satisfaction that comes from moving forward and overcoming obstacles. 'I smashed that bug,' wrote Tom in his diary. He is a programmer and had been working to fix a bug in the software he was creating. 'The bug that had been frustrating me for almost the whole week. That may not be an event to you. But I live a very drab life, so I am all hyped. No one really knows about it. Three of the team members who would be involved are out today, so I have to sit here rejoicing in my solitary smugness.'

Tom's is one of nearly 12,000 diary entries from 238 employees from seven different companies that Teresa Amabile, a professor of business administration at Harvard Business School, collected to study how the work environment can influence motivation. Tom's great day at work was a symbol of the main discovery of the study, which analysed those thousands of diary entries. They called the discovery the 'progress principle'.

What Amabile and her colleagues discovered was the power of small wins. According to her, 'Of all the things that can boost emotions, motivation, and perceptions during a work day, the single most important is making progress in meaningful work.' Even the smallest step forward can lift your spirits significantly. Or in other words, perhaps one small step for the project may be one giant leap for happiness at work. These are always the best days at work. Conversely, analysis of the worst days at work shows the single most prominent cause is setbacks.

I like to apply the progress principle when I work on something big like a book project. Every day, I calculate how much progress I have made in terms of the word count. That helps me see a little progress and feel a small sense of achievement on a daily basis.

HAPPYWORK

❑ Consider whether your current job is lacking either bigger purpose (ask yourself, am I helping to make the world a better place?) or smaller purpose (is the function I have within my organization meaningful?). Is there anything you can do to change that?

❑ Explore volunteering or a work side hustle, not for additional income but for additional meaning.

❑ Create a Smile File. Gather all the testimonies you have received that show you are making a positive impact on the people you are working with and for.

❑ Practise job crafting. Is there another way to look at your job? Are there some meaningful elements you could add to or focus on in your current job?

❑ Record every bit of progress, no matter how small. The warm glow of accomplishment will help motivate you towards your overall goal.

FLAT, TRUSTING AND CONNECTED

I was at the bakery around the corner from my home the other day. Being a distracted researcher, I often forget things and this time it was my wallet, but I really needed a cinnamon swirl. It was kind of a hygge emergency. Thankfully, Freja was at work and she knows me quite well. She will sometimes start to make the coffee I drink when she sees me parking my bike outside. So the missing wallet was no issue – she knew I would be back tomorrow.

It's a simple illustration of how trust makes life easier. A lubricant that allows transactions and interactions to flow more smoothly. It helps that they know my name and I know their names and a little about them. Freja's dad works at the hospital. Signe at my local café dislikes you ordering with your earphones in, and my local fishmonger will give a free fish cake to customers' kids.

Trust is what defines not just Denmark but the Nordic quintet – that and our love of pickled herring, of course. Denmark, Sweden, Norway, Finland and Iceland all enjoy high levels of trust. There is trust towards neighbours, the police and the government, and between managers and employees. Danes trust their workplace managers to do the right thing, and leaders trust employees in return. You are expected to take responsibility and do your job, without anyone looking over your shoulder.

According to the European Social Survey, Danes are the most trusting people out of thirty-six European nations. Trust was measured using a simple question: Do you believe you can trust most people – on a scale from 0 to 10, where 0 is 'You can't be too careful' and 10 is 'Most other people can be trusted'. Denmark has an average score of 6.92, followed by the other Nordic countries.

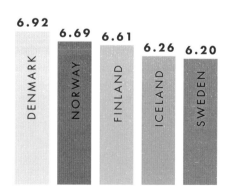

DENMARK	NORWAY	FINLAND	ICELAND	SWEDEN
6.92	6.69	6.61	6.26	6.20

'We have something absolutely remarkable and unique in Denmark in terms of our unheard-of high level of trust towards each other. It makes our society richer,' says Gert Tinggaard Svendsen. 'It allows us to not control and monitor each other all the time. And control is expensive. Really expensive.'

I meet Gert in a small café around the corner from the Happiness Museum in Copenhagen. He is a professor of political science at Aarhus University in Denmark and perhaps the world's leading expert in trust. His motto is: 'Control is good. Trust is cheaper.'

'I got into this because when I was a young man, in the 1990s, I went to the US, to the University of Maryland. My supervisor, Mancur Olson, was asking me all these questions, like why do Denmark and the other Nordic countries perform so well in economic and social terms? I had no good answers. I also got to meet Douglas North – the Nobel laureate in Economics – who similarly started to quiz me about Denmark. He and others were interested in what they called the Nordic puzzle. Did Denmark have some secret resource? A secret sauce? In the end I got annoyed! I had come to the US to study – and all they wanted to know about was Denmark.'

After Gert returned home, these questions continued to haunt – or inspire – him. He wondered if the key to the Nordic puzzle might be somewhere that economists rarely look. It was not in raw materials in the ground or the education between people's ears – it was something between people. He developed the theory that it was trust. 'We have an exceptionally large pool of trust in the Nordic countries,' he says.

It is why you will notice babies sleeping outside in their prams while their parents are inside a café, enjoying a coffee. It is why you will see unmanned stands by the roadside laden with berries, fruits and vegetables. You just leave the money in the jar or make a transfer with your phone.

Trust matters for happiness – because it makes your everyday life easier and it makes you worry less – but it also has a positive effect in the workplace. Now, the Nordic countries enjoy some of the highest levels of trust in the world and that is a privilege, but there are trustworthy people all around the world – and far more of them than we imagine. When researchers measure trustworthiness, they will sometimes leave wallets with cash in them and an ID card or the phone number of the owner and see how many wallets are returned with the money still in them. The biggest study dropped 17,000 wallets around the world – and on average 50 per cent of the wallets were returned with the money intact. Interestingly, when people are asked what percentage of the wallets they think would be returned with the money still in them, they usually underestimate it. So perhaps it would be worth trusting people more than we do. At least in the workplace there can be a high payoff. But what exactly is the return on investment when it comes to trust?

The Return on Investment of Trust

Employee: 'Hey, boss, you look a little tired. Are you getting enough sleep? Are you experiencing a bit of stress?'

Boss: 'No, no, I am fine. Very fine. Very productive.'

Employee: 'That's great, boss. By the way, did you hear about the study by Professor Astrid Richardsen from a Norwegian business school, looking at almost 3,000 managers?'

Boss: 'Yes, but I would love to hear your take on it.'

Employee: 'What she found was that the level of trust a manager has in their employees is a predictor for whether the manager will be diagnosed with stress. Professor Richardsen believes that managers who trust a lot are better at delegating and thereby reducing their own work and stress load.'

Control may mean that a couple of slackers work harder, but it may also mean that the majority of people, who resent the control and the mistrust, decide to work less.

According to *Harvard Business Review*, studies show that when companies choose to trust their employees, their productivity and the quality of their work increase. So, it is not just managers who benefit from trust.

Comparing people in high-trust companies with people in low-trust companies, researchers have noted:

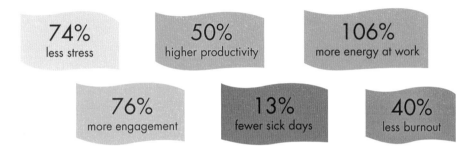

74% less stress

50% higher productivity

106% more energy at work

76% more engagement

13% fewer sick days

40% less burnout

And people in high-trust companies enjoy their jobs 60 per cent more.

Perhaps that is why 88 per cent more of the people in organizations with high trust levels would recommend their place of work to family and friends – and why 50 per cent more of them plan to stay with their employer in the next year.

In short, there are a lot of upsides to working in a high-trust organization – and a lot of reasons for companies to want to build trust.

This isn't new information to many organizations though. In 2016, PwC (Pricewaterhouse-Coopers) ran a survey of global CEOs and found that 55 per cent think that lack of trust is a threat to their organization's growth. However, the majority have done nothing or very little to increase internal trust levels in their respective organizations. Perhaps it is because they don't know how or where to start.

Okay, so trust is great – but how do we get it? How do we build trust?

HAPPINESS TIP: FIVE WAYS TO BUILD TRUST IN THE WORKPLACE

1. Be honest. The fastest way to destroy trust is to lie. Being honest is a fundamental step in building trust. If you have done something wrong, say so. If you don't know the answer to a question, ask for help. I find people mostly respond positively when I admit I don't know something.

2. Listen with empathy. In order for people to trust you, it is vital they feel that you hear, see and understand them.

3. Value your long-term relationships. Build and maintain long-term relationships and connections. Facilitate opportunities for employees to connect and build relationships with one another. Take part in activities that can drive a sense of belonging and togetherness.

4. Honour your commitments. If you say you are going to do something, do it. If you don't keep your word, trust will erode. In smaller organizations, the sanctions might be greater if you don't honour your commitments. Maybe this is one of the reasons for the higher levels of trust in Denmark. It is a small community, with a population of 5.9 million people and spanning only about 350 kilometres by 450 kilometres – you are likely to be bumping into the people with whom you went to school. So, if you don't keep your word or you act dishonestly, you are more likely to face social sanctions.

5. Give it time. Trust is built over time and leads to the belief that someone will act in a supportive manner in a given situation – it provides a sense of security when dealing with others.

The Flat Pyramid

We have seen there are some things you can do to build trust in your workplace, but it is much easier to cultivate trust in what we call 'flat' organizations.

According to the *Global Competitiveness Report* by the World Economic Forum, Denmark has some of the flattest work hierarchies in the world – if not the flattest – out of almost 140 countries. This means that no matter what your position or your job title is, you are encouraged and entitled to speak your mind and express your views. The thought behind this being: if your opinions are not heard when decisions are being made, then why should you care about those decisions? You are on a first-name basis with everyone – even your boss, of course – but it can often be difficult to spot the boss in the office.

My friend (and tennis arch-rival) Ib recently told me of an episode at work that exemplifies what this looks like in practice. It was his new non-Danish colleague's first day and they were having lunch together with some other co-workers in the canteen. They all worked in IT. A guy in a Hawaiian shirt joined them. Bold move in a nation that wears black every day, except for occasionally dressing up in a flamboyant grey. So, the group started teasing the guy. 'How was the surf this morning, Brian?' 'Did you bring pineapples for lunch again, Brian?' 'Laundry day, is it, Brian?' That sort of thing, I imagine. The next day, there was a big announcement and the entire company gathered to hear the CEO speak. The guy who had been wearing the Hawaiian shirt the day before – now wearing a suit – took to the stage. He starts

speaking. 'Who is that guy?' Ib's new colleague asks him. 'That's Brian, the CEO,' he replies. 'No, seriously, who is he?' My friend's new colleague could hardly believe that the CEO would not only have lunch with his employees but would also tolerate being teased. In Denmark, having lunch together with your co-workers and your boss is considered normal. You do not eat alone sitting in front of your computer. It works to connect people and it is a great equalizer.

Former Danish prime minister Poul Nyrup Rasmussen once said that it is rare to see a Dane with a knife in one hand without a fork in the other. Dark joke, I know, but honestly, who doesn't like to eat? Lunch at work in Denmark, however, is just as much about connecting with co-workers over non-work topics – and creating a sense of community – as it is about tucking into a delicious pickled herring on rye.

Perhaps the importance of lunching together across the hierarchy is most evident when it disappears. One of my good friends, who did not grow up in Denmark but worked for a major Danish company with several thousand employees, had always thought it was so cool that the CEO would have lunch in the canteen. He would sit at a random table and chat with people about work and life. He would get insights into every corner of the business, and the employees felt that they were all on the same level and could easily talk to the CEO. However, the CEO moved on and a new guy took his place – and suddenly the CEO was nowhere to be seen. He never came to the canteen, he was having lunch by himself in his office. The atmosphere in the organization started to change. It felt more hierarchical. My friend left the company soon after. He is one of the brightest people I know, and one of the hardest-working, and any organization should do their very best to keep people like him.

Power Distance

I am sure that when that new CEO started eating lunch in his office, Denmark rose a point on the indexes measuring power distance. Power distance is defined as the extent to which less powerful members of organizations within a country expect and accept that power is distributed, or to put it in Monty Python terms, the 'You're not my king – I didn't vote for you' scale.

This is a metric used to measure the degree of inequality that exists – and is accepted – between people with and without power. A high score indicates that a society accepts an unequal, hierarchical distribution of power, and that people understand 'their place' in the system. In a survey conducted by Hofstede Insights, countries scored as follows:

Denmark **18**
Iceland **30**
Norway **31**
Finland **33**
United Kingdom **35**
Germany **35**
The Netherlands **38**
Canada **39**
USA **40**
Italy **50**
Japan **54**
Spain **57**
Czech Republic **57**
Greece **60**
France **68**
Poland **68**
Bulgaria **70**
India **77**
China **80**
Ukraine **92**
Russia **93**

Perhaps the flattest organization in Denmark is the Copenhagen-based construction company Logik & Co., which has existed since 2002. There are no bosses. All the employees decide on the strategy of the firm together – they are the top authority and jointly discuss whether to tender for projects, which materials to use and who should be laid off if the company is struggling financially. In such a situation, some employees might volunteer to be sent home, or they might all decide on a collective pay cut. Oh, and everybody is paid the same, whether they are a carpenter or the bookkeeper. They employ about fifty-five people and have a turnover between 60 and 80 million Danish kroner – on average around £8 million. They are known for their social responsibility and often employ people who have experienced unemployment in the past.

This might seem out of this world to many, but it's a great example of how workplaces can function when they have all of the components that I'm exploring in this book – trust being a key one. So although it might seem unlikely that you'll ever experience a workplace as equal as this, maybe you're a business owner who could take inspiration from it – or perhaps you will be one day. If we want to work like the happiest people in the world, we have to believe it is possible.

I Get High (Job Satisfaction) with a Little Help from My Friends

Okay, so flat hierarchies with a high level of trust contribute to your happiness at work. But we need one more ingredient to populate those hierarchies: good people. When we ask people directly what makes them happy at work, the most frequent answer is: my colleagues. Perhaps with good reason. A lot of us see more of our co-workers than we do of our family – so getting those relationships right is key to being happy at work.

There is a crucial question that you need to ask yourself on this subject: do I have a best friend at work?

And we are talking *best* friends here. Not 'yeah, I had a beer with Mark from accounting one time' but full-on Frodo and Sam, Calvin and Hobbes or Charlotte Lucas and Elizabeth Bennet – or me and pancakes for that matter. A best friend is of course someone who wishes you well, who has your back and helps you deliver that report into the fires of Mount Doom.

According to a *Harvard Business Review* article featuring data collected by Gallup, if you have a best friend at work you are more productive, healthier and – most importantly for this book – more satisfied with your work.

It makes good sense that you would be happier at work with a best friend by your side – but I find it surprising that people with a work best friend are much more engaged in their work than those without one. If I was working with my best friends, we would work less and talk more about how twenty years ago we went on a four-day hike in Sweden with nothing but a kilo of rice, a saxophone, a guitar, two air rifles, a tent and a bottle of chilli garlic sauce. On day two we were hallucinating about cake. Oh, and do you remember the hike where Mikkel's shoe caught fire? But I digress – back to work!

According to Gallup, women are more than twice as likely to be engaged in their work (63 per cent) if they strongly agree that they have a best friend at work compared with those that don't feel that way (29 per cent).

Unfortunately, only two out of ten employees in the US would say they have a best friend at work, and companies are thus losing out. Gallup calculates that if six out of ten people felt they had a work best friend, organizations could harvest 12 per cent higher profits, 36 per cent fewer safety incidents and 7 per cent more engaged clients.

6/10 people feel they have a work best friend

12% higher profits

36% fewer safety incidents

7% more engaged clients

Not only is feeling more connected to your colleagues on a personal level good for the company, it could also result in greater happiness in the long term for you too. People move on and companies go belly up, but some friendships are for ever. The added benefit of having a best friend or friends at work is that you may be able to bring them with you after work is done, whether you leave your current job, retire or get laid off. Several of my current friends are people I've met through previous work positions.

In addition, the importance of friends when it comes to staying the course goes beyond work. We are social creatures and more likely to stick to certain things – like sports, education and work – if we feel part of a team. One small piece of evidence for this is the fact that the Duolingo language-learning app – which millions of people across the world use – reports that learners who follow their friends are 5.6 times more likely to finish their language course. They track each other's progress and congratulate each other when they reach milestones. *Que interessante, no?*

You might be sitting there thinking, 'Great, I have some mates at work, lucky me! Now I can really appreciate how important they are,' or perhaps you're thinking, 'Crap, maybe that's why I'm struggling at work. Maybe I'll start prioritizing the social side a bit more rather than just getting my head down,' or 'I've tried to make friends here but they really aren't my sort of people, so maybe it's time to think about whether this is the best place for me.' We often don't put that much importance on the social aspect of our jobs and tend to think of making friends at work as an added bonus, whereas the research shows it is fundamental to how well you can do your job, as well as how much you enjoy it, which is equally important in my book.

Let's look at the other factors that affect how we feel about our jobs . . .

Are You Likely to Leave
Your Company Soon?

According to Gallup, these are twelve of our most important wellbeing needs as employees. Go through and respond with a 'Yes' or 'No', and if you say 'No' to a lot of these questions, you are likely to want to leave soon. So you might want to consider whether you can influence any of these aspects of work, so you can turn a 'No' into a 'Yes', or it might be time for you to consider whether this job is good for you. We all need to be better at putting ourselves and our happiness first.

		YES	NO

1. I know what is expected of me at work.

2. I have the materials and equipment I need to do my work right.

3. At work, I have the opportunity to do what I do best every day.

4. In the last seven days, I have received recognition or praise for good work.

5. My supervisor seems to care about me as a person.

6. There is someone at work who encourages my development.

7. At work, my opinions seem to count.

8. The mission or purpose of my company makes me feel my job is important.

9. My associates or fellow employees are committed to doing quality work.

10. I have a best friend at work.

11. In the last six months, someone at work has talked to me about my progress.

12. In the last year, I have had opportunities at work to learn and grow.

HAPPINESS TIP: START WITH WHO

Imagine you could create a team with all the greatest people you have worked with in the past. Back in 2011, I started a magazine called *Fotorama*. I was really interested in photography and enjoyed visiting exhibitions and reading about photographers and their trade. But all the available magazines were less about photography and more about cameras. I thought there should be a magazine where you could get an overview of upcoming photo exhibitions, read about photojournalism or the history of photography, and learn how to paint with light. Screw it, I thought, let's create one ourselves.

I knew a few people that would be perfect to help me create this fun project. Lise is a great writer, Lana and Anne Sophie are talented art directors and Michael had great experience in sales – luckily, they were all excited about the idea too. After a few months of creating content and pitching for support, we managed to get 3,000 magazines we distributed to cafés around the city. We made three issues before I went on to create the Happiness Research Institute and spend all my time on that. It was so rewarding to make something from scratch and I got to do cool stuff with my friends. What's not to like?

So, imagine if you could gather five of your best friends – what skills do you possess? What could you build? What are your shared interests? Or what ludicrous idea can you come up with that could unite even more people behind a common project? Did you know that the largest snowwoman ever, according to Guinness World Records, was built by the residents of Bethel, Maine? She was 122 feet, 1 inch tall. She didn't fully melt until July! What a cool way to gather a community.

The Order of the Elephant

One way to make friends is of course to make people feel appreciated. That can be done in different ways.

A couple of years ago, I saw a large bell by the exit in a supermarket. Above the bell was a sign saying, 'Chime the bell if you feel that you have got great service, so the employees can feel appreciated.' It was a nice thought, I suppose. However, Danes are essentially a nation of introverts who do not like to draw attention to themselves. We will gladly wait for minutes behind you in the supermarket as you decide which milk to get instead of saying, 'Excuse me – could I just grab this one.' So, ringing a big bell in the supermarket – that is just not going to happen. Out of curiosity, I waited thirty minutes to see if people would ring the bell. No one did.

Organizations tend to place the responsibility for recognizing employees on the managers – which is important too – but this overlooks that we also need to be and enjoy feeling recognized by our co-workers. So-called peer-to-peer recognition schemes can be a quick and easy way to increase our sense of recognition and accomplishment – and perhaps also boost the BFF level at the office.

The best programmes I've seen have the following shared characteristics. They are:

Specific: Instead of 'Job well done,' say, 'I really like how you handled that situation where the patient vomited and you made her feel better about it, you even made her laugh.'

Immediate: Show your recognition today, tomorrow or this week – not in a performance review six months from now.

Fun: It should be something that we all want to be part of. Like smashing a piñata.

Inclusive: If there are only one or two people who keep getting the recognition, that is likely to breed resentment and the feeling of being overlooked. Try to include everyone in the programme. We all have successes that should be celebrated from time to time.

Public: It should be clear and public who is being recognized.

I heard about a workplace with a system that I think ticks many of these boxes. The Order of the Elephant – or, in Danish, Elefantordenen – is Denmark's highest-ranking honour. Originating in 1693, it is now almost exclusively used to honour royalty and heads of state. However, a group of Danish nurses have created their own version. They use a small toy elephant, pinned to your uniform, to recognize each other's great work. If you are currently wearing the Order of the Elephant, you get to pick which of your colleagues has done excellent work this week and award it to him or her, then they wear the elephant next week and pick the next recipient, and so on. It is immediate and public, and toy elephants are by definition fun.

How to Build for Connection
– the LEGO Way

There is something else we can do to make the social fabric at the office stronger: thoughtfully designing the office space. On this subject, I think it's worth learning from what LEGO has done.

You are probably familiar with LEGO, one of the world's leading manufacturers of play materials based on the iconic brick, founded in 1932 by Ole Kirk Kristiansen in Billund, Denmark. If you have read my earlier book *My Hygge Home*, you may already be aware that I am a total fanboy, and that LEGO is short for *'leg godt'*, which means 'play well'. But not only do they play well, they also work happy. LEGO tops the lists of the world's most reputable companies and is one of the biggest toy businesses in the world with more than 25,000 employees in more than forty countries – and it has some of the happiest employees.

Job Index is the biggest job-search site in Denmark and it collects data on joy at work among Danish companies from current employees. LEGO has come top of the class several times. Across parameters like management, career opportunities, collaboration and relationships, LEGO earns five stars. In short, everything is awesome. So, what is it that it does so well?

Firstly, it has created a workspace that allows employees to thrive as a community and to work in all kinds of different ways. It has been playfully designed – of course – to be an inclusive environment that fosters collaboration across the team to develop the best play experiences for kids.

We are talking meeting rooms with glass-topped tables with drawers full of LEGO underneath, giant dinosaurs made of LEGO, a huge LEGO waterfall and the 15-metre 'tree of creativity' – the largest LEGO build to date. The idea of play and having fun is central to the company.

So, dinosaurs, waterfalls and giant trees – great, you may say, but we are a small start-up with a tiny budget compared to LEGO, with its turnover of billions. But I have good news for you: there are still a lot of lessons to learn from the thought that LEGO has put into creating the best possible conditions for their workers. For example, their research shows both that we enjoy the flexibility to work from different places depending on our mood and what task we have to do, and that we need a sense of belonging at work – that we enjoy having a work tribe and knowing the people we work with. 'Hi, Mikkel – how was the camping trip? Oh my god, what happened to your shoe?'

According to Anne Sofie Fedders, who is LEGO's Head of Ways of Working, you need to understand how your employees actually work and what their different routines are like. She heads a team of internal experts that includes psychologists and anthropologists and has been involved in designing the new LEGO HQ in Billund – LEGO Campus – where 2,000 people work.

At the HQ there are various 'neighbourhoods' of about 100 people. There is no fixed seating, but you can sit with the people you know and work with. Each neighbourhood has a council that includes managers and employees who figure out together how to best design the neighbourhood to fit the needs of the people actually using it.

One of her key pieces of advice is: be an anthropologist. Don't ask: What should we do? – but ask a lot of detailed questions: What is the first thing you do in the morning? Where do you grab your coffee from? Where do you go for a break? What happens in a typical meeting? Where do you take phone calls? How do you collaborate with co-workers?

The LEGO Campus has different areas for different activities. Depending on whether you need to brainstorm with colleagues, answer emails or concentrate on how to optimize a production line, you may need different environments. But the anthropological approach also helped the designers understand that people's moods will impact on where they choose to work within the building.

Anne Sofie points out that it is important to make sure employees also feel a sense of belonging. So, you want to have flexibility in your workspace – but you also want to work close to people you know. The LEGO building is divided into different zones – the red zone is focused on creativity, the blue zone is focused on problem solving.

You don't typically have your own desk (though you can, of course, if that suits you best) but you have a team area where you can choose one of the desks. This is because, while LEGO understand that flexibility may be good, they know we also like to have a sense of belonging. You simply can't compute connecting with all the 1,999 other employees on the LEGO Campus.

There is a space that is quiet, a space covered with plants, and a place that feels like a busy café with the barista machine noise and music. Because some days you need to sit quietly in the corner by yourself, and some days you need to have energy buzzing around you.

Ride into the Friendship Zone

There are several studies that show how being friendly with your colleagues benefits both you and your company, but I think my favourite is 'Prosocial Bonuses Increase Employee Satisfaction and Team Performance', conducted by five professors at Harvard Business School, Duke University, Liège University and the University of British Columbia. It explored whether making sales teams more social would impact their sales performance. The researchers randomized the teams, and, in some teams, people were given €15 each and told to spend the money on themselves. In other teams, people were also given €15 but were instructed to spend the money on a randomly selected teammate. Everyone was also asked to spend the money by the end of the week.

The people who spent the money on themselves bought sportswear, small items of jewellery, food, alcohol and CDs. (Yes, the study is more than ten years old.) And the people who were asked to spend the money on another member of the team bought gifts like books, wine, plants, a stuffed animal, a piñata, and one paid a teammate's sports league fees.

The sales teams in question were in the pharmaceutical industry, and they would try to get doctors, pharmacies and hospitals in Belgium to buy certain drugs. Each month, the teams' sales performance was measured. What the researchers found was that the teams that spent money on each other – or as they refer to them in the study, the prosocial teams – sold more of their products than the teams that only got money for themselves.

The researchers could then calculate the return on investment for the money the teams had received as a personal or prosocial bonus. They found that all the teams performed better. However, the teams that had spent money on themselves sold €3 more for every €10 they had received – so a net loss. Meanwhile, the prosocial teams sold €52 more for every €10 that were spent on someone else. In other words, the prosocial teams smashed it – the sales and the piñata. At the Happiness Research Institute we have taken inspiration from this and gone ice skating, played pétanque, and sailed around in the canals of Copenhagen. Whether it is time or money, or both, investing in your team as a whole is the key to a happy, successful workplace.

In the modern-day management literature classic *Top Gun 2: Maverick*, the team of pilots that Maverick oversees are fiercely competitive and not working well together. In response, Maverick organizes a game of touch football on the beach for some fun and teambuilding (it had nothing to do with pandering to the fans of the iconic volleyball scene in the first movie, of course).

So, when your boss asks you why you have taken your team to a ball game on the beach – you of course channel your inner Maverick, who answers, 'You told me to build a team. Here is your team.' In a perfect world, 'Playing with the Boys' would then suddenly start coming through the office intercom as you walk out the door. Speaking of bosses, being able to avoid the bad or even toxic ones is also key to experiencing happiness at work.

Avoid Toxic Bosses

One study by the UKG Workforce Institute included 3,400 people across ten countries. It found that managers have just as much of an impact on people's mental health as their spouse. And both managers and spouses have a bigger impact than people's doctors and therapists. In addition, according to the study, 70 per cent of employees would like their manager to do more to support their wellbeing and mental health. In addition, 81 per cent of people say they would prioritize good mental health over a high-paying job. And 64 per cent say they would be willing to take a pay cut for a job that better supports their mental health.

70%
of employees would like their manager to do more to support their wellbeing

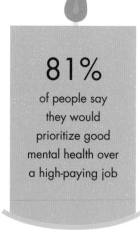

81%
of people say they would prioritize good mental health over a high-paying job

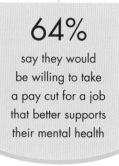

64%
say they would be willing to take a pay cut for a job that better supports their mental health

Your boss is going to have a huge influence over how happy you are at work. They have influence over almost every aspect of your job. Don't kid yourself that your boss is going to change their ways. They are not. If your boss is a jerk, you should quit. It doesn't have to be tomorrow. You may need to secure a new job first. But you need to quit. You may even choose to do it on 31 March – which is International Quit Your Crappy Job Day.

It's said that people don't leave jobs, they leave managers, the data seems to support this. According to research by Totaljobs, 49 per cent of people in the UK have left a job because of their manager. This is why it is important to understand your future boss before you say yes to a new job, which we will look at more closely next.

HAPPINESS TIP: HOW TO SPOT
A GOOD BOSS IN AN INTERVIEW

❑ I will stay in my current job for life. It ticks all the boxes in terms of purpose, freedom and the rest of the factors that we are exploring in this book. But it also gives me an additional layer to experience everything with. For example, when I visit a new city, I automatically start to consider how the urban design impacts quality of life. That is a privilege. The only downside is that I will probably never again be on the applying end of a job interview – hoping they would ask me this one question: 'Describe yourself in three words', and I would answer, 'Lazy.' Just to check if they have a sense of humour.

❑ But if you are looking for a new job, you should be aware of the following red flags in terms of your potential new boss's behaviour:

❑ They talk only about their own success. Bad bosses take all the credit. Great bosses celebrate their employees' successes and talk about them. And take note if they talk about their own accomplishments more than they ask about yours.

❑ They talk more than they listen. Good managers are open to great ideas, no matter where those ideas come from.

❑ They act differently around their own managers, being polite to the boss and inconsiderate to their staff.

❑ They treat staff poorly. Observe how your interviewer interacts with the people they manage if you get the chance. Or if you happen to meet over lunch or coffee – how does they interact with the staff at the restaurant or café?

- They don't seem interested in the non-work aspects of you. The best managers are curious about you as a human being from the start.

- They don't admit mistakes. The best managers are honest about their flaws and their company's shortcomings. Ask them to tell you about when they've failed and how they recovered from it or what they would most like to change about their company or leadership style.

- If they 'demand too much of themselves' or describe themselves as 'a perfectionist', then consider whether they might also demand too much from you.

- They micromanage. Almost nobody will admit they do this but perhaps you can get an idea of where they sit on the micromanager scale by asking questions like 'How often would you like to be updated on project progress?' or 'How often do you schedule check-ins with your current staff?'

- They give you a bad gut feeling. I think this is the most important one. Trust your intuition. Do they make you feel insecure? Did they interrupt you or did they let you speak? Did the interaction make you feel more or less confident that you could do the job?

HAPPYWORK

- ❑ Make your co-workers feel appreciated. See if you can find a way to do it that is SIFIP: Specific, Immediate, Fun, Inclusive and Public.

- ❑ Find a work buddy. If you do not already have a BFF at work, consider who has the potential to be your wingman and put a bit of time into getting to know them better. It sounds obvious but it could make a huge difference to your happiness at work.

- ❑ Consider what you can do to level the hierarchy in your organization. Talking to and getting to know people outside your team or department is a good way to start.

- ❑ Mark 31 March – International Quit Your Crappy Job Day – in your calendar. If you have a toxic boss, then tomorrow is 31 March. You can't change your boss's behaviour but you can change your boss.

- ❑ Consider a project outside work – one that is centred around great people. Whether your project would be a new photography magazine or building the world's biggest snowman, who would you pick for a team that would be fun to work with?

- ❑ Get to know your local shop owners. The first step in building trust in your neighbourhood is getting to know people and letting people get to know you. Start with their name. See if, in the next week, you can learn the name of at least three people in your neighbourhood: your fishmonger, baker, barista or whoever foams your milk.

CHAPTER

4

——

THE PURSUIT
OF FREEDOM

Eggs for breakfast, or toast? Each day you make choices and decisions. Some are small and some big. You probably try to go for the option that you believe will give you the most happiness, balancing short-term pleasure and convenience with long-term happiness. Now imagine your freedom stripped away. I bet you're pretty riled up and ready to go full Braveheart with blue paint and a kilt, aren't you? With good reason. Freedom impacts your quality of life – and even the length of it.

In 1976, a group of psychologists in Connecticut conducted what has now become a somewhat famous experiment in a nursing home. The Arden House was rated as one of the best care units in the area and offered high-quality medical attention, recreational facilities and comfortable surroundings. In the experiment, residents on one floor of the home were given the freedom to choose and care for plants and to decide which day of the week would be movie night. *King Kong*, anyone?

On another floor, residents did not get to make these choices. When the experiment began, the first group of residents was no healthier or happier than the second group, but they soon began to show more activity, greater alertness and a better mood. Eighteen months later, they were still doing better than the second group of residents – and with a mortality rate of 50 per cent of the second group. In the almost fifty years that have passed since that study, evidence of the relationship between happiness and autonomy has continued to grow.

Autonomy is the ability to make your own decisions about what to do, rather than being influenced by someone else or told what to do. This covers everything from deciding how a task is done, to when you work and from where, and it might be one of the reasons why Danes experience a high level of happiness at work. Employees of Danish organizations typically experience high levels of autonomy. In fact, Denmark ranks highest amongst twenty-seven European countries in terms of employee autonomy. A prime example of how this plays out comes from one of the world's oldest amusement parks.

The 3-Metre Rule Rules

_____

In the heart of Copenhagen lies Tivoli Gardens, which first opened in 1843. Pre-pandemic, almost five million guests visited the amusement park each year. That is a lot of 'Wheeeeeeeeeeee!'

Around 3,700 people have Tivoli as their place of work during the year. These employees might serve 300 portions of candyfloss in a day, check the safety bars on the rollercoaster or greet the thousands of guests. However, what unites them all is that they all follow the same '3-metre rule'. The rule means that you are the CEO of everything within a radius of 3 metres. No matter where you are and no matter who you are, that is your responsibility. If you see litter within your 3-metre radius, you pick it up, if you see a guest looking for something, you stop and ask them if you can help. You follow the rule whether you are the vice president or you serve coffee.

For every single employee, their focus is on four concrete elements:

1. Being a host for the guests

2. Solving the guests' problems

3. Keeping the gardens clean

4. Being the best colleague

How these elements are fulfilled is up to the individual. Being the CEO of your immediate radius provides a lot of autonomy.

The 3-metre rule is a language tool. It is easy to communicate and easy to remember, but it also gives a great sense of empowerment, responsibility and autonomy. There is no fixed script or manual. *How* you are a good host to the guest and make them feel welcome is up to you. Every morning before the park opens, the different teams gather and talk about how the previous day went and whether or not they feel guests are likely to have had an excellent experience.

This contrasts somewhat with the hotel check-out experience I had when I visited Atlanta for work a couple of years ago.

'Thank you for staying with us, Mr Wiking. Did you enjoy your stay, Mr Wiking?'

'Yes, thank you.'

'We hope you will stay with us again next time you visit Atlanta, Mr Wiking.'

Somewhere there was a manual, where these sentences had been carefully drafted in an attempt to let the guest feel valued. However, it only made me feel alienated and underlined that I was far away from home.

The Tivoli approach, letting the employees decide for themselves how to perform their tasks, seems to work. When surveyed, 94 per cent of the park's guests said they would 'definitely' or 'likely' recommend Tivoli to others and were satisfied or very satisfied with their visit. The employees also seem to enjoy being the CEO of the 3-metre radius. Nine out of ten agree with the statement: 'All in all, Tivoli is a good place to work.' Empowered employees serve customers better.

Flexibility Is More Than Working from Home

Fortunately, autonomy doesn't only happen in Tivoli. As we saw earlier, draw an organization chart of any Danish company and it is basically just one horizontal line. Danish workplaces are very much flat hierarchies, and employees *and* employers have an egalitarian mindset. Employees expect to be consulted and heard when decisions are made about their jobs or workplace – and they expect to be in charge of exactly how their work should be done and when. This high level of autonomy is usually paired with a high level of flexibility.

The good news is that it is not just in Denmark that autonomy and flexibility lead to more happiness at work. When we examine the share of employees with a 'high' level of job satisfaction in each country, broken down to reflect the amount of flexibility within their work, we find, unsurprisingly, that more flexibility is always better. Data from Eurostat displayed on the next page shows that employees with a high level of flexibility are always more likely to feel a high level of job satisfaction.

What is more surprising is that, in a lot of countries, having a high degree of flexibility trumps working from home. I think this is an important point. A lot of people do not have the opportunity to work from home due to the nature of their work – but this doesn't mean that we can't harness the positive effect of flexibility. It is not working from home that is the source of joy – it is, for instance, the ability to leave work for an hour or two to let the repairman in on Thursday afternoon, or working on a schedule that suits your needs.

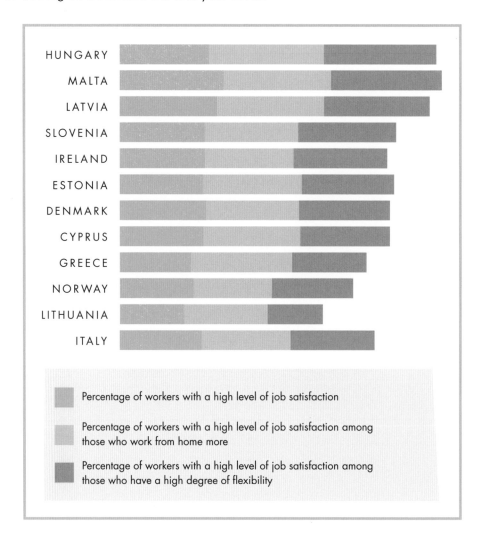

Percentage of workers with a high level of job satisfaction

Percentage of workers with a high level of job satisfaction among those who work from home more

Percentage of workers with a high level of job satisfaction among those who have a high degree of flexibility

Look for Flexibility

If you are looking for a new job, make sure to ask what flexibility looks like in practice, and consider whether that suits you. In Denmark alone, a flexible workplace can be interpreted as anything from the opportunity to work from home once a week or month to 'come to the office whenever you feel like it'.

Here are five questions that will help you shed light on the level of flexibility in the organization:

WHAT IS YOUR WORK CULTURE LIKE?

CAN YOU TELL ME ABOUT ONE OF YOUR CURRENT EMPLOYEES WHO ENJOYS A LOT OF FLEXIBILITY?

WHAT BENEFITS ARE FOCUSED ON WORK–LIFE BALANCE?

WHAT'S THE COMPANY POLICY ON WORKING FROM HOME?

DO EMPLOYEES HAVE A SAY IN THE STRUCTURE OF THEIR GOALS AND TASKS?

Or, if you are afraid to ask, look instead for clues about their work culture. One Danish company that we worked with at the Happiness Research Institute embraced the idea of failing forward. They saw the acceptance of failure as a stepping stone to success. They lived the mantra that if you are not making mistakes you are not innovating. So, they had a fridge full of champagne and celebrated when a mistake had been made.

And if you are considering which career path to pursue in order to maximize freedom and autonomy, then – according to Monster, the major job search site – the best jobs for people who love to work autonomously include accountant, HR specialist, IT support, graphic designer, artist, consultant, research scientist, marketing manager, purchasing specialist and teacher.

Gotta Have Some Faith in the People

Boss: 'But people can't deal with all this freedom! It will be chaos!'

You: 'I am not sure, boss – did you hear about Spotify's WFA programme?'

Boss: 'Waste, Fraud and Abuse?'

You: 'No, boss – Work From Anywhere.'

In February 2021, Spotify launched their Work From Anywhere programme. No more going to the office ever – unless that is what you want. As this was Spotify, I assume that they did the announcement while blasting George Michael's 'Freedom' at the office.

So, did everybody just pack their bags and move to the Bahamas, Chiang Mai and Narnia? Not really. When Spotify evaluated the programme a year after they had launched it, of the 6,500 employees who could now work from anywhere, just 150 people, or around 2 per cent, had moved to a different country. Among those working in the US, around 300 people moved to a different state (the majority of those from New York to New

Jersey). Meanwhile, six out of ten people continued to use the regular office as their main place of work.

Both employees and companies recognize that there are some benefits to working in the office. A learning point for Spotify has been to encourage their teams to meet in person at least every six months. The reason for this is the understanding that trust – which facilitates cooperation – is created faster when people meet face to face.

At the same time, Spotify benefited from the WFA programme in various different ways. First, they got access to new talent pools as many of their new hires came from places outside their main hubs. Second, they were able to retain more of the existing talent in the company. Compared to similar companies, Spotify had a lower turnover of employees while the rest of the world started to talk about the Great Resignation. Or, in the words of the Great HR Prophet George Michael: 'I won't let you down . . . / 'Cause I would really, really / Love to stick around, oh yeah.' But of course, flexibility doesn't have to mean Working From Anywhere – it could be something as simple as the freedom from being stuck in meetings.

Freedom from Interruptions

One of my favourite initiatives when it comes to increasing both productivity and happiness at work is the 'Tuesday Morning Quiet Time' initiative that the American tech company Intel has experimented with.

The ambition was to secure four hours of concentration time for employees. A block of time in which people could tackle difficult, complex tasks that require a stretch of uninterrupted attention, instead of trying to get it done in the seventeen minutes between two meetings, and those nine minutes between two phone calls, and so on. So, on Tuesday morning between 8 a.m. and noon, the company sent phone calls to voicemail, email servers were shut down and no meetings were scheduled.

When measuring the effect, Intel found that the trial, which lasted for seven months, had been 'successful in improving employee effectiveness, efficiency and quality of life for numerous employees in diverse job roles'. Of those participating, 71 per cent recommended extending it to other departments.

Thinking Outside the Boss

The ultimate level of freedom is perhaps being your own boss. Some people start companies because they can't help it, some because of a great idea that needs to materialize, and some due to frustration with their existing workplace. You know what they say: if you have to beg for a seat at the table, maybe you should build your own. And some people start working on their own because they believe it will make them happier. The data seems to suggest that they might be right.

Across several studies, we have found that self-employed people are happier – both with their work and with life overall. However, there are some important caveats. It matters *why* you became self-employed. Did you choose it yourself – or were you not able to find a regular job and being self-employed was your only option? Also, does self-employment make people happier or are happier people more likely to become self-employed? Maybe happier people are more optimistic – my business is going to do great, they think – and therefore they are more likely to set up shop. Well, the good news is that we can follow people over time and see what the cause and effect are when it comes to happiness and being your own boss.

What we see is that being self-employed has a different impact on your happiness depending on where you live in the world. Entrepreneurs or self-employed people are happier in Europe, North America, Australia, New Zealand and East Asia compared to full-time employees. However, in Latin America, the Caribbean and sub-Saharan Africa, the reverse is true.

I am part of the first statistic. It has now been more than ten years since I first had the idea of starting a think tank on happiness. One late September day in 2012, I was stuck in the office working at a think tank on sustainability, and I stumbled upon something called the *World Happiness Report*. It had just been published by the United Nations, following a 'happiness resolution' that had been passed the year before, asking all the countries of the world to focus more on happiness and see what they could do to improve quality of life. The report gave an overview of happiness research and included a ranking of more than 150 countries' levels of happiness. In the top spot was Denmark. That was not the first time I had seen my home country being in first place when it came to liveability or quality of life or similar rankings. 'Why?' I asked myself. 'Why is Denmark – along with the other Nordic countries – always doing well in these happiness rankings? There should be somebody looking into this. Somebody should start a think tank to look into happiness in Denmark.' And then I thought: 'Maybe . . . I should do that.'

The idea of working on understanding what makes some people happier than others, and what we can do to improve quality of life, got me really excited. I lay awake at night thinking about different angles to study. How does the way we design our cities impact our wellbeing? What policies could be implemented to improve happiness? How do age, income and education impact your happiness level? There were so many dark areas on the map and I wanted to go explore them. Preferably to the theme tune of *Indiana Jones*.

But 2012 was in the wake of the great recession. You could still hear the echo of the bursting real-estate bubble and the crash of financial markets. Starting a new company in this climate seemed risky – and this wasn't only a new company, it was a crazy idea. A think tank on happiness.

However, there were a couple of things that pulled me in the direction of the crazy idea. First, I was very inspired by the mantra that you should try to be a person not of success but of *value*. And I thought there would be a lot of value in looking at happiness from a scientific perspective. And second, I was faced with a memento mori. My mentor, who was fifteen years my senior and who I looked up to in many ways, had been diagnosed with a terminal disease at the age of forty-nine. And many years previously, my own mother had died when she was forty-nine – and that made me think: 'What if I only live to see forty-nine?' In 2012, I was thirty-four, which would give me fifteen more years. What should I spend those years doing?

I could continue in my current job, which was fine, stable and paid a good salary – but I wasn't passionate about it any more. Or I could embark on the crazy, wild and fun journey I imagined working as a happiness researcher would entail. Two months after the thought had first occurred to me, I had quit my job and started out with what I thought was a good idea and a bad laptop. But third, what enabled me to do that was savings. I had been making decent money for the past five years and I had lived relatively frugally. The simple maths was that my bank balance had been going up, and it was now at a point where I could continue with my current, relatively modest lifestyle for two years before those savings would be gone. That gave me two years to pursue the dream. I have since been informed that such a stash of savings is also known as 'FU money', squirrelled away ready for the day when you can finally tell your boss you've had enough and walk out with the rest of your life ahead of you. I didn't realize it at the time, but I had been building up my own Freedom Fund.

Why You Should Have a Freedom Fund

Whether you call it FU money or a Freedom Fund, it gives you the option to quit your job if you are not happy with it. You don't actually have to quit, but the money will give you leverage in negotiations. Take the example of Jim Collins, the American financial writer who popularized the term FU money. When he was a young man, he had saved up some money to travel around Europe for a month. When he asked his boss for a month's sabbatical (in Europe we call it a holiday), the boss thought about it and said no. 'Well, you know,' said Jim, 'I'm going to do it anyway, so I guess I quit.' 'Well, wait a minute,' said the boss. 'All right, you can have the sabbatical.' The point of the story is, of course, that having FU money empowers you in negotiations and makes you bolder.

It also works as insurance. You may love your job now. You enjoy it and your boss is great. They see you and support you. But what you don't know is that they are thinking about leaving – and then the jerk parade starts. A series of toxic bosses comes along and soon your happiness at work melts away. It may be time to turn your side hustle into a full-time gig or to change your regular job.

This is another area at which the Danes excel, and I think it's worth taking inspiration from them. Compared to people in most other OECD countries, the Danes switch jobs quite frequently – and this might be a source of happiness at work. Don't like your job? Quit. If we look at salaried workers only, rather than those on an hourly rate, the average Dane spends 7.2 years with one employer before they switch jobs. Italians spend 12.2 years on average, the French 10.8 years and the Germans 10.2 years.

One of the reasons for this is the Danish labour market model – the 'flexicurity model'. Briefly explained, this is built on two core elements. The flexibility part means that employers can hire and fire at will, without high costs for layoffs. The security part is the fact that you receive quite good benefits if you are unemployed. The unemployment insurance fund means that you can get two years of unemployment benefits while you search for a new job – then you are switched to the lower subsistence payments. Currently, the unemployment benefits are up to the equivalent of £2,300 per month. Remember, taxes and the cost of living are high in Denmark, so that may sound better than it is. Nevertheless, Danish unemployment benefits are, from an international point of view, very generous. This safety net allows Danes to more easily leave a job that is not making them happy; they have the freedom to quit.

Well, that is great, you might say. But I live in a country without such benefits. So, that is why we need to build you that Freedom Fund, which can also work as an emergency fund. Emergencies are part of life. Some days are good, some days are bad, and life throws us curveballs from time to time. That is part of the human experience. I look a lot at happiness data where people are followed over decades, and there is no one who does not experience setbacks from time to time. We know they will come – from layoffs to getting sick – so we need to prepare. One factor that seems important in differences in people's happiness levels is whether they can cover an unforeseen expense of around £1,000 without having to borrow money.

Unfortunately, the average savings in countries like the UK and the US is worryingly low; 40 per cent of people in the UK do not have enough money to support themselves for a month in the absence of their usual income and are living from payday to payday, while almost one in ten have no savings whatsoever. A lot of people are struggling to make ends meet and building an emergency fund may be out of reach. However, for those for whom an emergency fund is doable, it is strongly advisable.

One way to add to your Freedom Fund is to reduce your food waste. The average UK family with kids throws out food worth £700 each year. What if each year you took that £700 and put it in the stock market, instead of in the bin? The stock market goes up some years and down some years – and while past performance does not predict future gains, of course, let us say that it continues to increase by about 8 per cent on average. Well, in twenty years the £700 would have grown to around £14,000. But with the magic of the eighth wonder of the world – compound interest – it will have become £32,033 after twenty years, which is coincidentally roughly the median British household disposable income, or £79,298 after thirty years.

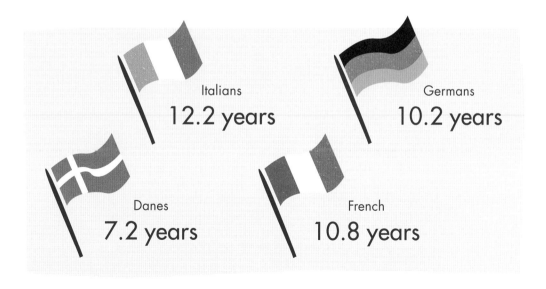

Italians
12.2 years

Germans
10.2 years

Danes
7.2 years

French
10.8 years

HAPPINESS TIP: THIRTEEN WAYS TO BOOST YOUR FREEDOM FUND

1. Get rid of your car. Cars are one of the biggest expenses in most people's lives. Consider walking, biking or taking public transport instead.

2. Cook your own meals. Eating out is expensive. Cooking your own meals is not only cheaper but also healthier and more fun.

3. Buy secondhand. Charity shops, car-boot sales and online marketplaces are great places to find deals on everything from clothes to furniture.

4. Cancel subscriptions. Do you really need that streaming service or magazine subscription? Cancel anything you don't use regularly.

5. Shop for groceries strategically. Buy in bulk and plan your meals around what's on sale. Avoid buying expensive processed foods and stick to basic ingredients that go a long way, like fresh and tinned vegetables, pulses and rice.

6. Reduce your energy usage. Unplug electronics when you're not using them, turn off the lights when you leave a room, use a clothesline instead of a dryer, turn down the heat when you're not at home, and consider switching to LED bulbs.

7. Sell stuff you don't need. Make some extra cash by selling items you no longer use, like clothes, books and electronics.

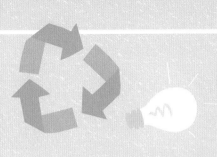

8. Do your own home repairs. YouTube has plenty of tutorials on basic home repairs. Save money by doing it yourself instead of hiring a professional.

9. Invest in quality, not quantity. Don't waste money on cheap, disposable items that will need to be replaced frequently. Instead, invest in high-quality items that will last.

10. Use public amenities. Parks, libraries and community centres offer free entertainment and resources. Take advantage of them!

11. DIY entertainment. Host games nights, movie nights and potluck suppers instead of going out. You'll save money and have fun with friends.

12. Take care of your belongings. Proper maintenance can extend the life of your possessions. Take good care of your clothes, appliances and electronics to save money in the long run.

13. Use round-up services. These round up the total to the nearest pound every time you spend and put the difference in a savings pot. When you buy groceries for £15.25, 75p goes into your savings without you having to do anything.

Retire on FIRE

Of course, the ultimate freedom that we are all working towards is retirement, and although it's easy to bury your head in the sand about how many years lie ahead of you at work, the better you plan for it the sooner that day will come.

Some have taken the Freedom Fund idea to new heights with the FIRE option. FIRE is an acronym for Financial Independence Retire Early, an apt name for a plan that essentially enables you to go full Braveheart.

The idea behind FIRE is to live really frugally, saving and investing at least 50 per cent of your income, with the goal of living off the passive income those investments will generate. One of the thought leaders in the FIRE community is a fellow Dane, Jacob Lund Fisker, who published *Early Retirement Extreme* in 2010. He lives in the US on around $7,000 per year and retired at the age of thirty-three. His ability to live on so little comes from the fact that he is quite the Renaissance man – he likes to do everything himself instead of buying goods and services. For example, he makes his own washing powder. But other members of the FIRE community are less extreme.

'Once I learned that formula of early retirement, to me, intead of spending $18 on a glass of wine in a bar, spending $18 on a box of wine at home and having your friends over made way more sense,' Bianca DiValerio says. 'You're still able to do the same things – you just kind of change a little bit of the facets to them.'

Bianca started working as a flight attendant when she was twenty-two, became financially independent at forty and retired at forty-four. That is quite an accomplishment in itself – but especially considering that Bianca lost everything in 2008 when the financial crisis hit. At the time, she had three investment properties that she had to sell for less than she owed.

In 2016, Bianca heard about the FIRE movement and started tracking every cent that she spent. The first year she cut back on everything and lived super-frugally.

'Basically, in an airport a crappy salad was $8 – but if I made the salad myself with salmon and all these delicious things, it was about $3 to $4.'

She bought her used Honda CRV for $9,000 in cash from Craigslist, and walked dogs with a service that allowed her to get her dog walked for free when she was away working. Her total expenses in that first year were $18,297, and working extra hours with her long experience allowed her to save the 77 per cent of her income she had left after that: $61,719. And interestingly, it is not the size of your income that determines when you can retire, it is your rate of savings. Someone who makes £50,000 per year but also spends £50,000 per year will never be able to retire – while someone who makes £40,000 per year and spends £30,000 per year should be able to retire after a thirty-two-year career. The following table assumes 5 per cent returns during the years you save – and a safe withdrawal rate of 4 per cent. We will get to that in a second.

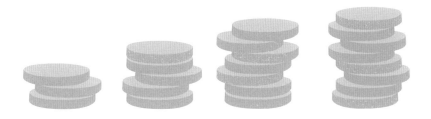

HOW SOON CAN YOU RETIRE?

PERCENTAGE OF INCOME SAVED	WORKING YEARS UNTIL RETIREMENT
5	66
10	51
15	43
20	37
25	32
30	28
35	25
40	22
45	19
50	17
55	14.5
60	12.5
65	10.5
70	8.5
75	7
80	5.5
85	4
90	Less than 3
95	Less than 2
100	0

A common rule of thumb in the FIRE community is the 4 per cent rule. This is based on the Trinity study, where researchers explored what would historically have been a safe withdrawal rate in order to never run out of money in a thirty-year retirement. So how much money can I take out of my investments each year and never run out of money? What they found was that if people took 4 per cent out of their investments each year they should have a very high probability of not outliving their money during a thirty-year retirement. Bianca's FIRE number is $650,000, so, based on this rule, Bianca can take up to $26,000 out each year to cover her annual expenses.

To figure out how much you would need to have invested according to the 4 per cent rule, you need to tally up your annual expenses and multiply the total by 25. So, £10,000 of expenses per year would mean a nest egg of £250,000 invested. £50,000 of expenses needs £1.25 million invested. That is, of course, an astronomical amount for most people – and some people in the FIRE community opt for the 'barista fire option', which means working part-time and letting their investments cover 50 per cent of their expenses, for instance. However, the belief that each expense has to be matched by an investment 25 times greater means that people pursuing FIRE focus a lot on reducing their expenses. A £5 coffee every day costs £1,825 over a year, which would need £45,500 to be invested to cover it according to the 4 per cent rule. Many people find it easier to just cut that out.

'I am not saying this is attainable for everybody,' says Bianca. 'It is not easy. You have to delay gratification, and we are not in a society that delays gratification any more. But I am saying there is something that everybody can do for their retirement, and the first step is to track your expenses.'

Reaching financial independence may have simple formulas – you can find ways to earn more, spend less and invest the difference – but implementing these can be very hard. However, I am impressed with the level of creativity when it comes to side hustles to earn extra income: dog walking, filling out surveys, tutoring, working as an extra in films, propagating plants, hosting international students or renting out rooms, transcribing podcasts and becoming a mystery shopper. If it happens to make a bit of money and then some more, you may consider taking the leap if the flexicurity fund is in place. You never know, you might just create the job of your dreams. But I think the most important element in all this is that you have to know what enough is – and when enough is enough. There will always be a higher number, so I recommend considering how your everyday life would change with, say, £100 more per month. Would it reduce financial worries and allow your kids to take those swimming lessons? Then surely that will impact your happiness. But if the extra £100 per month is just going to give you a more expensive red wine in your glass, then it might not move the needle when it comes to your overall satisfaction with life.

Although the ultimate goal of all this is to never work again, I think it is interesting that when you look at the FIRE community in the US and the UK you see that once people have enough money to retire, most of them don't. They write books, start their own businesses, make music, consult, volunteer full-time in disaster relief, paint or help people renovate their houses. Some of these activities pay and some of them don't.

Retirement doesn't always mean lying on a beach sipping margaritas all day, even if that's what you worked towards your whole life. The first week or perhaps even month it might be nice to decompress and do nothing, but soon after, most people get restless – and also, those little cocktail umbrellas get up your nose.

In fact, it seems that when people are able to quit their jobs due to having enough money coming in through investments to cover their expenses, some of them experience symptoms of depression after the first movement of 'Ode to Joy – I never have to work again' has passed.

At the Happiness Research Institute we are currently involved in a five-year study called Seniorklar ('Senior Ready'), looking at the relationship between work and happiness among 14,000 senior citizens in Denmark. The early findings show that people who continue to work after the traditional retirement age are happier and less lonely. However, at the time of writing we are still uncertain of the causality. Surely, if people are suffering from health challenges, that will reduce their happiness and their ability to work after retirement age. So poor health leads to lower levels of happiness and earlier retirement. But maybe it is a two-way street – maybe continuing to work after retirement also leads to high levels of happiness. There is already evidence that suggests it does. Among the people who are beyond retirement age and continue to work, 43 per cent say work gives them a sense of purpose and 35 per cent say they enjoy feeling useful and productive.

Similarly, Pete Adeney, who is essentially the cult leader of the FIRE movement, says his best days are when he accomplishes stuff – gets difficult tasks done, lifts heavy weights, goes for hikes, does carpentry – while his worst days are spent doing nothing sitting around the house.

'I've learned that work is an incredibly powerful source of happiness. The key is that it must be creative, social and engaging work that brings you towards a purpose you believe in.' He holds that work is better when you don't have to do it for the money. The ultimate freedom at work is having the option to not do it.

Pete's view echoes the findings of one of my favourite studies: 'Time Use and Happiness of Millionaires – Evidence from the Netherlands', published in the journal *Social Psychological and Personality Science* in 2019. The study looks at how the very wealthy spend their time and how this relates to happiness.

First of all, it turns out that millionaires spend more time on active leisure, for instance, exercising – like waxing their jet, I suppose – or volunteer work, as opposed to passive leisure, such as relaxing and watching television. And second, millionaires spend more or less the same amount of time working as the rest of us do. The main difference is that more of the work of millionaires consists of tasks they have control over.

Wealthy people decide *what* to do and *how* to do it for 93 per cent of the hours that they spend working, compared to 76 per cent for the general population. But for both groups, job autonomy was positively related to life satisfaction.

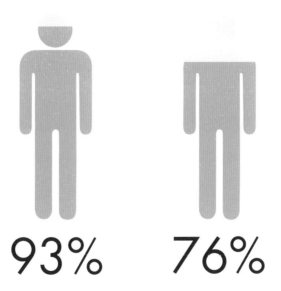

93%   76%

So, freedom at work is good for happiness. Check. But how you get to work also matters.

Freedom Has Two Wheels

Remember the study that Daniel Kahneman undertook, asking the participants about what they did the day before and how those activities make them feel? The worst daily activity was the morning commute, and the evening commute was third worst. However, the commute does not have to be a drag. The important thing is to ensure your commute enables you to move your body in some way – whether that's walking, jogging, scooting or cycling.

Nine out of ten Danes own a bicycle – and if we look at Copenhagen, 62 per cent of people cycle to work. In fact, the majority of members of parliament cycle to Borgen. Together, the cyclists of Copenhagen cycle more than 1.2 million kilometres every day.

From a happiness point of view, an active commute will beat a passive one any day. Several studies show that both cycling and walking put us in a better mood than driving. One study, by a group of researchers at McGill University in Montreal, examined which kind of transportation is best for our mood. They looked at 3,400 people and examined six typical means of transport: going by car, bus, train, metro, bicycle and on foot, during summer and winter.

The study also looked at the satisfaction gained from several aspects of the journeys, and from this the researchers calculated one overall satisfaction score for each mode of transport. What they found was that cyclists and pedestrians have the highest overall trip satisfaction, report that their life satisfaction is most impacted by their

commute, and have the highest overall life satisfaction, while those who had to drive or take the bus were the least satisfied. Metro and train users fell in between.

Another study, 'Does Active Commuting Improve Psychological Wellbeing? Longitudinal Evidence from Eighteen Waves of the British Household Panel Survey' – the rule of thumb for academic papers being the longer the title, the better – by researchers from the University of East Anglia, followed commuters over time to understand what happens when you change your form of transport. Studying a group of 18,000 people in the UK, the researchers found that people who switch from driving to walking or cycling experienced improvements in psychological wellbeing – even if the new trip took *longer*.

Everything is in walking distance, if you have the time. But jokes aside, the distance you have to travel to your work of course influences whether you can walk or bike there. Around 46 per cent of working Danes live 10 kilometres or less from their place of employment, and 29 per cent are 5 kilometres or less away. Both distances are certainly doable on a bicycle.

Being on a bicycle gives me a sense of freedom. Especially when I am passing all those cars stuck in the morning traffic. In the Copenhagen rush hour, biking is often the quickest way to get to work – and you are also free from the stress, hassle and cost of finding a parking spot for your car. Cars run on money and make you fat – bikes run on fat and save you money. Maybe your job is too far from your home to bike to work, but walking or cycling instead of driving to get groceries could be an option to reduce car use.

In the UK, the average motorist spends £218 each month running a petrol or diesel car, *not* including car-finance payments, while the average household spends roughly £1,100 a year on car purchases and financing, representing 4.3 per cent of their annual family budget. Imagine that going into your FU fund instead.

HAPPYWORK

❑ Start tracking your expenses. How much do you actually need each year to live the life you currently live? It will help you start asking questions like, do we really need HBO, Netflix, Disney Plus and Amazon Prime all at once, which cost £460 per year, or could we alternate between the four, cutting the cost to roughly a quarter? Remember cheap is pronounced frugal.

❑ Start building your Freedom Fund. 'But I like my job!' you may say, and well, that is great. But what if that changes? Five years from now, your great boss might leave and start her own business and Jared, who talks about his Porsche a lot and how he is training for the Ironman this summer, thinks it would be great if you have that report done by Monday at 8.

❑ Consider what side hustle you would find enjoyable. It doesn't have to be something lucrative, just something you think is fun and which you have complete control over.

❑ Explore whether it would be feasible to introduce initiatives like the 3-metre rule or Tuesday Morning Quiet Time at your workplace.

❑ If you are looking for a new job, bring the five flexibility questions to the interview, or if you are considering a career change, investigate what different career paths will look like in terms of flexibility.

❑ It is time to dust off your mood booster of a bike – and if you work too far away to commute by bike, consider looking for another job or relocating. This is not achievable for everyone, especially if you have kids. But if you can get within biking distance of your workplace, drop your car commute and even your car. It will make you richer, healthier and happier.

CHAPTER

5

THE WORK–LIFE
BALANCE MYTH

In Chapter 1, I mentioned the Japanese word 'karoshi'. The term was first invented in the 1970s to describe deaths caused by work-related stress or a brutal office culture.

In 2015, a young woman working for Dentsu, a Japanese advertising agency, jumped to her death. The firm was fined for violating working standards as she was forced to do more than 100 hours of unpaid overtime each month – and the CEO of the firm resigned. Both the government and Dentsu have since created initiatives to mitigate *karoshi*, such as having the lights in the office automatically turn off at 10 p.m. in an attempt to force the employees to leave, and the government has made it mandatory to take at least five days of holiday per year. Still, despite Japanese workers having twenty holiday days per year, on average ten of those days are left on the table and never used. Still today, several hundreds of *karoshi* incidents are reported and there is suspicion that instances are underreported and that the actual number is much higher. What started as a Japanese phenomenon is now a global issue, and it is undermining our health and wellbeing.

A landmark study by the World Health Organization in 2021 found that each year 745,000 people die from stroke and ischaemic heart disease (also known as coronary heart disease) as a direct result of having long working hours – defined as at least fifty-five hours a week. That is an increase of 29 per cent since 2000, showing that overworking is a serious public health issue the world over.

The effects that long working hours have on your health and longevity are both direct and indirect. The first is the price of chronic stress, with elevated blood pressure, and the indirect is how overwork affects other parts of your life – like sleeping less, exercising less (if at all) and eating less healthy food, as well as smoking and drinking more, which in turn affect your health.

The 2021 WHO study used a decade-long lag period to monitor and capture the health effects of overwork over time. Death by overwork doesn't happen overnight.

That is a good thing – it gives you the opportunity to do something about it before it is too late.

Some people around the world take drastic measures to avoid working long hours. It was more than five years ago, but I still remember the conversation I had in Seoul with a man in his early twenties, over lunch at a happiness-at-work conference. He was one of those people in whom you instantly sense an impressive level of intelligence. He was helping out at the conference, still at university and yet to embark on his career, so I was curious to know what he wanted to do work-wise. He leaned in across the table as though he was about to share the nation's top secrets.

'I want to go to the US,' he said. 'It does not matter which field. But I believe tech is the best bet if I want to emigrate.'

'And why do you want to leave Korea?' I asked.

'I want a better work–life balance than I can expect here. I know you in Europe have a five-star work–life balance, and the US may only have three stars – but here we have no stars.'

Sadly, the data backs him up. According to the OECD – the Organisation for Economic Co-operation and Development – in 2021 the global average for hours worked per worker each year was 1,716. The fewest hours were worked in Germany, Denmark and Luxembourg – and the most were in Mexico, Costa Rica and Chile. I can't help noticing a correlation between the number of hours worked per year and the levels of happiness. The happiest countries also seem to be the countries with the fewest work hours. No work is not good for happiness but too much work is not good either.

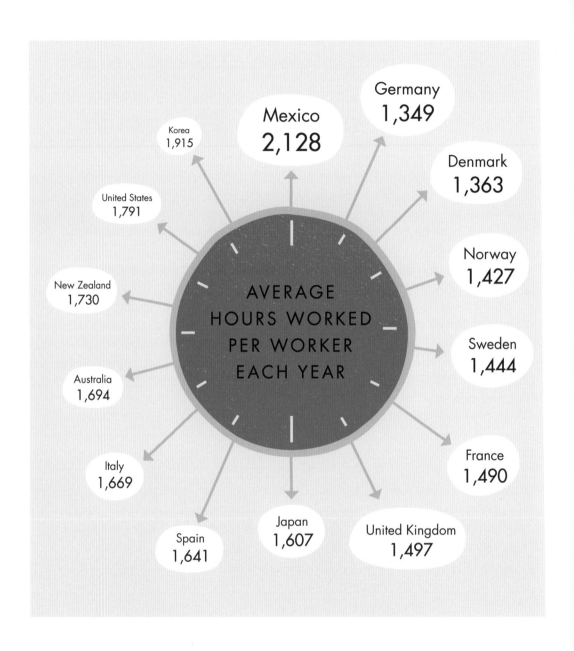

Korea
1,915

Mexico
2,128

Germany
1,349

United States
1,791

Denmark
1,363

New Zealand
1,730

Norway
1,427

AVERAGE
HOURS WORKED
PER WORKER
EACH YEAR

Australia
1,694

Sweden
1,444

Italy
1,669

France
1,490

Spain
1,641

Japan
1,607

United Kingdom
1,497

Work–Life Balance, Scandinavian-Style

When I speak to people who have moved to Denmark from the UK or the US, they often highlight the difference when it comes to work–life balance. The shift was perhaps best described by Cathy Strongman in the *Guardian* back in 2012, when she was living in Copenhagen with her family.

> *Our quality of life has skyrocketed and our once staunch London loyalism has been replaced by an almost embarrassing enthusiasm for everything 'Dansk'. The greatest change has been the shift in work–life balance. Whereas, previously, we might snatch dinner once Duncan escaped from work at around nine, he now leaves his desk at five. Work later than 5.30, and the office is a morgue. Work at the weekend, and the Danes think you are mad. The idea is that families have time to play and eat together at the end of the day, every day. And it works. Duncan baths and puts our fourteen-month-old daughter, Liv, to bed most nights. They are best buddies, as opposed to strangers who try to reacquaint at the weekend.*

I track her down online. Today, Cathy owns and runs a Pilates studio in Stavanger, Norway. Her husband's job led them from Copenhagen to Houston, then back to Scandinavia. Liv is now twelve and has three siblings. We talk about the difference in work–life balance in Scandinavia, compared to the UK and the US.

'There seems to be a greater respect for people's personal life and for their time in Scandinavia,' she says. 'And that people work on their own time. In London I might leave the office at 7 p.m. and Duncan could work until 10.30, but here work is much more condensed. You don't work less here, but you work more condensed. There is much more that 'it is your own responsibility and you do it on your own time' sense here. You get the work done – before 5 – and if not, then you leave work, go home, have dinner, and then you might work a bit later in the evening.

'If you are in a meeting in Norway and you get a call from the *barnehage* [preschool] and you need to pick up your kid, you leave and pick up your kid. If you are in London and you get a call from the preschool – you are in mad panic.' She sees how work invades people's time off: people on holiday talking work on the phone on the beach, people having to leave wedding parties because their work needs them. 'That would never happen here,' she says.

She also believes that people are more scared in the US and UK. Work dominates because of the fear of losing your job. You are more likely to take risks in Scandinavia because you know that the worst that can happen is not so bad. If you lose your job, you will not end up on the street. They may be far from perfect, but the social security systems in the Nordic countries do catch a lot of people when they fall.

That is why we should all care about unemployment benefits and why we should judge a society by how it treats its most vulnerable citizens. Because the fear of getting fired will make Brad, Belinda, Roger and Alice stay at the office until 8, making you look like a slacker if you leave at 7, even though you all finished your tasks by 5.

Maybe when the kids are older, they will move back to Copenhagen – but for now it is difficult to find another place that could offer them a better quality of life. Cathy loves teaching Pilates. Duncan's boss is one of her clients, who takes a class every week: an important break from work to take care of her health.

Cathy's story is just one data point, but it echoes what we see in the big data. For instance, the European Social Survey, an academically driven cross-national survey that has been conducted across Europe since 2001 and has data from thirty-eight countries, shows us that one of the biggest threats to our happiness is work infringing on our leisure time.

If you are too tired after work to enjoy things, if you worry about work problems when you are not working, if your job prevents you from giving time to your family or friends, that undermines your happiness on several fronts. It undermines your satisfaction with work, your satisfaction with life, how happy you feel overall and what kind of emotions you experience on a day-to-day basis. So, it is interesting to see what happens when companies experiment with a four-day work week.

Lessons from the Four-Day Work Week

Researchers from the Universities of Cambridge and Boston recently finished perhaps the biggest experiment around the four-day work week in the UK. It involved sixty-one companies and 2,900 people who worked for four days per week over six months.

The trial was a resounding success: less stress (39 per cent) and burnout (71 per cent) among employees, lower staff turnover (57 per cent), fewer sick days (65 per cent) and slightly higher revenue (1.4 per cent). What's not to like?

However, the study has some biases. The sixty-one companies that took part had all volunteered. Obviously, that influences the results – only companies that can already see the feasibility of a four-day work week for their organization would have signed up, and they would probably already have considered how it could be implemented. This may also explain why, out of the sixty-one companies that took part, fifty six of them – or 92 per cent – have continued the four-day work week, two of them are experimenting with other forms of a shorter work week and only three companies have returned to the five-day work week.

How to Get Five Days' Work Done in Four Days

In order to make it happen, the companies had to find ways to increase their productivity, which essentially came down to sending fewer emails (or emailing fewer people), disturbing each other less and cutting meetings. Or as Richard Branson, founder of the Virgin Group, has been credited with saying: 'A lot of time is wasted in meetings. Agendas get forgotten, topics go amiss and people get distracted. While some circumstances call for workshops and more elaborate presentations, it's very rare that a meeting on a single topic should need to last more than five to ten minutes.'

This trial provided some lessons we can all learn from to help us get more done in less time, no matter how many days we work per week.

Change the meeting culture – have fewer meetings, make them shorter and have a clear agenda for each meeting.

Implement 'focus time' daily, when you can work without interruptions.

Prepare a to-do list for the following work day – so you already know first thing what you need to focus on.

Think before adding people to an email. Just cc-ing them still means they get the email in their inbox and have to deal with it.

Automate. For instance, if you write an email to the Happiness Museum, you will receive an automatic reply with answers to some of the most frequently asked questions we get.

Involve as few people as possible in any given task.

And of course, there is no 'one size fits all' four-day week. Industries, organizations, structures and cultures are different. We need to look at different models. For instance, in a staggered model, employees alternate their days off to maintain a Monday–Friday schedule, while a decentralized model puts different departments on different work schedules depending on their needs, and an annualized system requires a worker's annual average to be thirty-two hours of work a week but doesn't specify a day off.

But what if your company is not flirting with a four-day work week – and moving to Scandinavia is not an option for you (perhaps you've seen those Nordic noirs and believe there is an alarmingly high murder rate here)? Well, there are still a lot of ways organizations can help improve the work–life balance. Perhaps one of the following might be feasible in your workplace and something you could suggest to your manager.

FIVE WAYS COMPANIES CAN HELP
WITH A BETTER WORK–LIFE BALANCE

1. Make use of leftovers. One company the Happiness Research Institute has worked with packed leftovers from lunch for employees to take home – so the workers didn't have to make dinner when they got home and the company reduced their food waste. Win-win!

2. Provide flexible work arrangements. Flexible working hours, remote working or job-sharing allow employees to balance their work and personal responsibilities.

3. Offer childcare assistance. Provide on-site or subsidized childcare services, to help working parents manage their childcare responsibilities.

4. Create communication guidelines. For instance, the company TaskUs has a policy called 'No Chat Weekends', which discourages employees from sending work-related emails and chat messages at the weekend.

5. Implement a manager-led culture shift. If managers leave early, take parental leave and don't send emails over the weekend, employees are more likely to tread the same path.

HAPPINESS TIP: HELP YOUR CO-WORKERS DISCONNECT

If you are like me, one of the joys of being on a plane – besides rising above the clouds and into the sunshine – is the lack of Wi-Fi, or at least this used to be the case. Not having access to my emails removed the pressure of having to reduce the number of red flags in my inbox, at least for the duration of the flight. Sometimes I will write or prepare a presentation – but sometimes I will just relax, read, listen to a podcast or AC/DC's *Back in Black* on repeat. Yes, I am that old. And I sense that I am not the only one who enjoys not having access to emails from time to time. For us AC/DC-loving people, it reminds us of a time when you would go to work and work, then leave work and not work. There was no just having a glance at the inbox, no just sending a quick reply.

The data backs this up, too; according to the Mental Health Foundation in the UK, 12 per cent of people who reported high levels of stress said that feeling like they needed to respond to messages instantly was a stressor. For all the benefits of living in a connected world, it is also a whole new source of work-stress that we have to deal with, the worst part being that it follows us out of work and into our personal lives.

But thankfully some companies recognize that their employees need downtime, relaxation and a chance to escape the constant avalanche of emails. Back in 2012, German car-maker Volkswagen decided to shut down their BlackBerry servers (remember, this was 2012) and blocked certain staff from accessing emails from evening time until the morning, so that people could watch DVDs or dance to 'Call Me Maybe' in peace without the ping of emails to distract them.

Today, unions in France, Germany and Ireland have won rights for workers to disconnect. For example, France has introduced regulations that set tighter boundaries around when a remote worker's obligations begin and end by setting out the hours when staff are not supposed to send or answer emails.

The challenge is, of course, that for some people it is helpful to be able to read and answer emails after 8 p.m. when the kids have been put to bed, so perhaps what we should aim for is the right not to feel obliged to answer every email as fast as possible, and to underline to our co-workers that we respect the way they design their work–life balance and boundaries.

Having an email signature like the following may be one way to start such a culture: 'I work flexibly & send emails outside normal office hours. There is no need to respond to my emails outside yours.'

Perhaps try this out and, you never know, not only could you feel less dominated by your inbox but you might just inspire someone else to do the same.

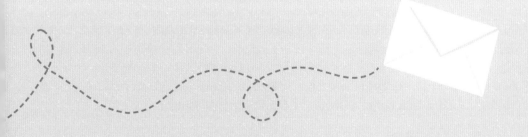

Beyond the Nine-to-Five:
Shared Housework

'I almost fell down the stairs when I read what you wrote me.' A connection on LinkedIn who was in town had asked whether we could meet to discuss a partnership. I replied that I could not because I was on paternity leave for the next six months. She could not believe my response.

I could not believe *her* response. But I know that I am the outlier here, and that it is a huge privilege to live in a society with so many family-friendly policies. Mothers and fathers are entitled to shared and paid parental leave in the Nordic countries. The period can be split between parents as they wish; thirty-nine weeks are allotted in total for this in Iceland, while new Swedish parents get a huge sixty-nine weeks per child. So there is a great big chunk to divide between the parents, and Nordic fathers therefore take more parental leave than fathers anywhere else in the world.

A common Nordic belief is that mothers and fathers should take equal responsibility for their children and that children have the right to be with both parents. But sharing parental leave also contributes towards a more gender-equal participation in the labour market, with fewer women stuck in unpaid work – and more equality at home. Men who take longer parental leave also do more unpaid housework, and spend more time caring for the child alone after both parents have returned to work – creating a fundamental sense of shared responsibility between parents.

However, it is not only good for women and kids if men take more parental leave – it is also great for the men. According to the report 'Shared and Paid Parental Leave – The Nordic Gender Effect at Work' by the Nordic Council of Ministers, there are studies from all over the world, including Denmark, that show that involved fatherhood improves the health status of men – they actually live longer. This has been dubbed the parental-leave effect. Men who take parental leave are more involved in the care of their children, have better relationships with them, communicate better with their partners about the needs of their children and have a better understanding of their children's and partners' daily life.

While Denmark still has some way to go in terms of equal pay for equal work and increasing the numbers of women in leadership positions, it does relatively well, along with the rest of the Nordic countries, when it comes to gender equality – at least according to the Gender Equality Index, as published by the European Institute for Gender Equality in 2022, featuring EU member countries.

GENDER EQUALITY INDEX

A score of 100 would mean that the country experiences complete equality between the genders.

EU average
68.6

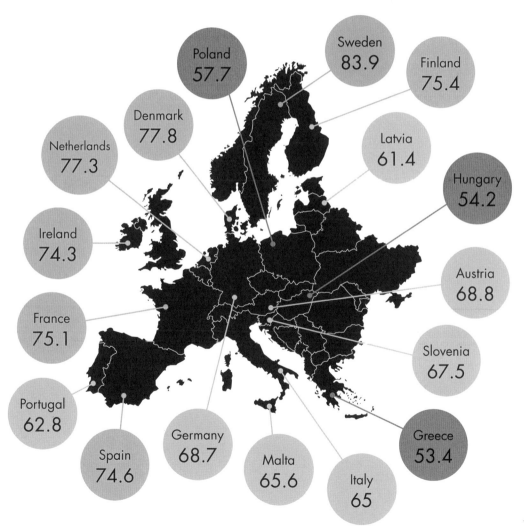

Poland
57.7

Sweden
83.9

Finland
75.4

Denmark
77.8

Latvia
61.4

Netherlands
77.3

Hungary
54.2

Ireland
74.3

Austria
68.8

France
75.1

Slovenia
67.5

Portugal
62.8

Germany
68.7

Greece
53.4

Spain
74.6

Malta
65.6

Italy
65

It should come as no surprise that countries with a high level of equality are happier. Double work – working full-time *and* taking care of all the chores in a household – is not a recipe for happiness. If you live with a spouse or roommates and you feel the workload at home is not divided fairly, it is time to have a chat about choreplay.

HAPPINESS TIP: BETTER CHOREPLAY IN SIX STEPS

1. Start by creating a list of all the tasks, chores and errands that need to be done in your household.

2. Go through each item on the list and consider who typically takes care of it. During the Covid lockdowns, many people realized just how much work goes into running a household as they could see what went on in the home all day.

3. Prioritize the tasks by considering which ones are essential for your household to function properly (such as cooking, cleaning and doing laundry) and which ones are optional (like redecorating a room). Are there any tasks that you consider nice but not essential (such as making the bed each morning) that could be delegated or eliminated altogether?

4. Discuss how each task should be done. For example, when it comes to dusting the living room, does it mean removing all the books from the shelves or would you prefer a quicker, less thorough approach?

5. Assign the tasks on the essential list. If there's a task that one of you enjoys doing, let that person take care of it. For instance, if you love cooking, it might feel less like a chore and more like a fun creative process for you.

6. Share the burden of the less-desirable tasks and consider whether any of them could be outsourced or combined with something you enjoy. For example, could you fold laundry while watching your favourite TV show to make the task feel less tedious?

Dugnadsånd – Raising the Bar(n) for Happiness

The daily chores are one thing but bigger projects are a whole other question. Whether you are painting your flat or building a terrace, we're talking about substantial work that we use our leisure time to complete and which seems to blur the boundaries between 'work' and 'life'. One way to make it more enjoyable, though, is to take inspiration from the traditional way of raising a barn in many societies.

Building a huge structure like a barn is a big project and requires more hands and muscle than is typically found within one family. So historically, calling on your local community to help out (unpaid) with raising a barn was common, especially in the US in the eighteenth and nineteenth centuries. Helping each other out through reciprocation made the whole community stronger, more resilient and, I would argue, also happier. Gathering friends or neighbours and turning the labour into a more enjoyable event meant building not only barns but also friendships.

The tradition lives on in the Amish communities but also, on a smaller scale, in many places in Denmark and the other Nordic countries. In Denmark, we would call this an '*arbejdsfællesskab*' – a 'work community' – and in Finnish, '*talkoot*' is the word for a gathering of friends and neighbours organized to achieve a task, something that may be a common good for the group and that cannot be accomplished by an individual alone. In Norwegian, there are the words '*dugnad*', meaning voluntary work done together with other people, and '*dugnadsånd*', meaning the spirit of *dugnad* – which was voted word of the year in Norway in 2004 and was used to help overcome the pandemic in 2020.

My friend Ida and her family have worked together in this way with two other families. Every year, each of the three families plans a big project, for instance to build an outdoor pizza oven, a chicken coop or a fence for the land where their sheep graze. Together, they complete the three projects, one in the spring, one in the summer and one in the autumn, on rotation. Each family makes sure the necessary materials and supplies are bought, and everyone brings tools. They work, eat and laugh together. Sounds like a great weekend to me.

Working together is much more enjoyable, the project is completed much faster, and it is also a great way to learn new skills from others.

So, don't be shy – invite people over to help you out with your project. There will be plenty of happiness in it for them, too.

From Work–Life Balance to Work–Life Blend

Back in 1999, I was working as a grape picker during the harvest at the J. Marquette vineyard in Champagne, France. I slept on a mattress on the floor above the press and in the morning Jacques Marquette would wake us workers with a loud '*Bonjour!*' After breakfast – a healthy dose of strong cheese – we would get in the back of the vans and drive to the fields, small strips of land around the village, and start filling our baskets with grapes.

Everyone would work with a partner, one on either side of the vine, one handful of grapes at a time. We would move all the way along a row, wait for the last pair of workers to finish, and then do it all over again. It was hard work, crouching down all day and sometimes cutting ourselves with the secateurs. But it was rewarding – it was evident that we were making progress with each snip of the secateurs. And when we returned in the evening, we would see the press in action and literally taste the fruit of our labour, then eat, drink and sing – before going to bed on the hard concrete floor, tired and happy.

I believe the harvest only lasted for about ten days, but my memories will last for a lifetime – I often think of those days working in the vineyard and feasting in the kitchen.

I think I was paid a total of around £200 or £300 for those ten days. Not a fortune, but also not nothing for a twenty-two-year-old. So technically it was paid work, but in retrospect it felt more like a holiday. This is why I dislike the term 'work–life balance'.

Putting the two in opposition to each other implies that work is not part of your life, and that life is the happy, peaceful antidote to your work. But we all know that it's not that simple. I think it makes more sense to aim for a 'work–life blend'.

Some of my most enjoyable days have been when work and life seem to blend. Whether that was harvesting grapes in Champagne or sharing a bottle of wine with my dad, looking at the floorplan for the upcoming Happiness Museum and discussing what to put in each room, or publishing the *Fotorama* magazine with a group of friends, or working on a side hustle with my buddy Jacob, attempting to import tea from Sri Lanka, or when I went to live in Spain for three months and wrote some really bad fiction. Some of the work paid, some didn't (pro tip: only import tea that people like) – but it all worked out to shape my skills, identity and memories.

There is work that is good for you and work that is bad, but I think it's wrong to label all work 'bad' and all of life 'good'.

My harvest experience is one of the reasons why I recommend taking working holidays, if you can. Working elsewhere is a great way to see the world, as it enables you to meet people, immerse yourself in a new culture, have life-changing experiences, all while earning your keep along the way. Perhaps your skills are valuable in other countries, like hairdressing, nursing or carpentry, or you could work in a bar or teach a language, or even a sport like skiing or surfing!

For some, it may be daunting to embark on a trip to work in another country. What about the taxes? Do I need a local bank account? And what about health care and work insurance? Fortunately, the Danish company ScandiMate offers services for craftsmen and -women who would like to work abroad. If you are a Danish carpenter, a Canadian log cabin might be something really cool to work on, for instance.

ScandiMate takes care of everything from plane tickets, work permits, travel insurance, accommodation, local bank accounts, tax codes and SIM cards for your phone. They send Danes to Australia, New Zealand and Canada. Why not find out whether a similar service exists in your country?

Embrace the Seasons

We experience different seasons throughout the year, and I think it's useful to remember that life has seasons, too – some will be busier and involve more work than others.

I've had seasons with a lot of work. I once did seventy-five interviews in forty-eight hours. I spent eighty days of one year travelling (including once having to sit on the back of a motorcycle to make it through traffic to the airport because I had one presentation in London in the morning and one presentation in Copenhagen shortly after lunch). I've been sorting name tags at 2 in the morning (the company I was working for was hosting a conference the next day with more than 1,000 delegates), only to discover that my co-worker was sorting by surname and I was sorting by first name. We worked more than 100 hours that week. It was tough – and it was fun. But I've also had seasons with no work and all play (mostly building LEGO and reading bedtime stories during my parental leave).

Maybe you can have it all – just not at the same time. Perhaps the key to a happy life is to embrace the seasons, the ebb and flow of work and life over a lifetime. And maybe it is time to abolish the idea of work–life balance and embrace the work–life blend instead.

HAPPYWORK

❏ Consider working abroad. Would another country offer you or your family a better mix of work and life? It does not have to be for ever, and a working holiday could be a way to test it out. Whether that is picking grapes for the harvest in France or working as a lumberjack in Australia, or something else. Grape pickers, lumberjacks or Doctors Without Borders – it is all good!

❏ Consider how you can get more work done in a shorter time by applying the lessons from the four-day work week experiment. If you don't think you should be in a meeting, ask the organizer whether it makes sense for you to be there or whether you might create more value for the organization elsewhere.

❏ Form an *arbejdsfællesskab*, or a *talkoot*, or a *dugnad*, or whatever you want to call it. Get four or so people or families to commit to one day or one weekend over the next year when you'll take turns helping each other out with some of the bigger DIY projects you dream of crossing off your to-do lists. You'll be more likely to complete them and they'll be more enjoyable in the process.

❏ Is the work at home not shared fairly? Have the talk about choreplay. Bring Post-its.

CHAPTER

6

—

REFRAMING

SUCCESS

Back in 2015, I spent a couple of months in Mexico. I needed to finish a book and could do that from anywhere – and okay, there might have been a woman in the equation as well. Anyway, this is where I first heard the following story:

> An American investment banker was taking a much-needed vacation in a Mexican village when a small boat docked, with just one fisherman and several fresh yellowfin tuna in it. The investment banker was impressed by the quality of the fish and asked the Mexican how long it took to catch them.
>
> 'Only a little while,' the Mexican replied.
>
> The American asked why he hadn't stayed out longer and caught more fish. The Mexican replied that he had enough to support his family's immediate needs.
>
> The American then asked, 'But what do you do with the rest of your time?'
>
> The fisherman said, 'I sleep late, fish a little, play with my children, take siestas with my wife, Maria, and I stroll into the village each evening to sip wine and play guitar with my amigos. I have a full and busy life.'
>
> The investment banker scoffed, 'I am an MBA from Harvard, and I could help you. You could spend more time fishing and with the proceeds buy a bigger boat, and with the proceeds from the bigger boat you could buy several boats until eventually you would have a whole fleet of fishing boats. Instead of selling your catch to the middleman, you could sell directly to the processor, eventually opening your own cannery. You could control the product, the processing and the distribution.'

Then he added, 'Of course, you would need to leave this small coastal fishing village and move to Mexico City, where you would run your growing enterprise.'

The Mexican fisherman asked, 'How long will this all take?'

The American replied, 'Fifteen to twenty years.'

'But what then?' asked the fisherman.

The American laughed and said, 'That's the best part. When the time is right, you would announce an IPO and sell your company stock to the public and become very rich. You could make millions.'

'Millions? Then what?'

To which the investment banker replied, 'Then you would retire. You could move to a small coastal fishing village where you would sleep late, fish a little, play with your kids, take a siesta with your wife, and stroll to the village in the evening to sip wine and play your guitar with your amigos.'

You may already be familiar with this joke, but I think we often forget the point of the story, which is that we sometimes get caught up in wanting more and lose sight of what is actually important to us. And while it may be easy to see the right choice in the joke about the fisherman and the investment banker, some of the choices in our own lives may be more difficult.

For instance, would you rather A) work forty hours per week in a job where you experience job satisfaction of five out of ten, can afford to eat out seven days a week, drive a Tesla, have your house cleaned by a professional, play golf at the weekends and go on two luxury holidays a year, or B) work forty hours per week in a job where you experience job satisfaction of ten out of ten, can afford to eat out once a month, take the bus to work, clean your house at the weekend, enjoy low-cost activities and take a budget holiday once a year?

I ask that question in a course I teach around happiness, and I find that usually about half the students choose option A and half choose option B. But what if we phrase it differently?

What if option B was you working forty hours per week in a job where you experience a job satisfaction of ten out of ten, are a great home chef and enjoy making delicious food each evening, you ride your bike to work and exercise every day, clean your house and go fishing or hiking at the weekends, and for your holiday you go camping by a beautiful lake in the woods, where you sit by the fire and teach your kids all about the constellations and their stories? When I frame the question like this, usually more people go for option B, about 70 per cent, while 30 per cent stick with option A. I am not saying that one is better than the other – people make choices based on what they think will bring them more happiness – but I think it is interesting how just a little reframing of option B moves people towards that alternative.

So, we may change our minds when we are presented with a great alternative and perhaps we all need to remind ourselves to step back and think about what we actually want rather than doing what we think we should do, or have been told to do. So many people assume that work won't make them happy and settle for an unrewarding job in order to pay for a bigger house and a nice car. But maybe it would be better to trade that fancy car for a not-so-fancy car – and instead take much more holiday. As a happiness researcher, I would certainly bet on more holiday making you happier than a luxury car – so maybe it is time to follow the Poul Principle.

HAPPINESS TIP: THE POUL PRINCIPLE

One of the organizations I worked for in my twenties and thirties was a think tank called Monday Morning. It attracted bright minds that often would challenge the status quo. One of them was Poul. What Poul did was not to ask for an increase in pay every year, like most of his co-workers; he would ask for more days off instead. He felt that he was making enough money to buy the things he wanted and additional income would not bring him additional joy. More free time, on the other hand, would. When I was working with him, he was up to twelve weeks of holiday per year.

The question is, should we be more like Poul? We can start by asking ourselves questions like: What would be worth more to me than a 2 or 5 per cent increase in pay? Is it one more day or one more week off a year? Is it not having to do evening shifts, or having 25 per cent of my evening shifts converted to day shifts? Or is there a skill I would like to learn, or a specific task that I would like to do less of or not at all, or something that I would enjoy doing more?

I often think that to be rich might mean having a lot of money – but to be wealthy means having a lot of time to live and enjoy your life. And the majority of guests at our Happiness Museum agree. We have asked them whether they would prefer to have double pay or double holiday time. Around two-thirds typically go with Poul and opt for the extra holiday.

The One-More-Million Syndrome

A couple of years ago, I was speaking at a conference at the Hotel d'Angleterre in Copenhagen. It was organized by a wealth management bank for the sons and daughters of billionaires. There were sessions on how to structure an investment portfolio, on future growth and on the relationship between money and happiness. That is where I came in.

I talked about how a lot of people suffer from the 'one-more-million syndrome' (or in their case, 'one more billion'). Believing that once they get to that level of net worth *then* they will be happy, and if they do get there and find themselves no happier, then more billions will surely do it.

Money does matter for happiness, don't get me wrong, but mainly because being without money is a cause of stress, worry and unhappiness. Not being able to put food on the table is undoubtedly not a happy situation. And people in well-paying jobs are happier and more satisfied with their lives and jobs than people who make less money.

With money, as with most things in life, we see diminishing marginal returns when it comes to happiness. Your first slice of cake is wonderful – slice number eight, not so much. It is the same with money. The first money you get is very important and will secure food on the table and a roof over your head. But if you are already making a lot of money and then you get more, you tend to spend it on silly things like a coat for your dog. In addition, people often care more about their relative income than their absolute income. How much money do I make compared to Karen in accounting, or the Joneses next door? I've been told that there is an American saying that a happy man is a man who makes $100 more than his wife's sister's husband.

'Your speech reminded me of one of my best friends,' said Liam, a member of the audience. Liam's friend had gone to the finest universities in the US. He became a lawyer in New York, making more money than his parents had ever dreamed of. One day, Liam asked him: 'What is the most important thing your parents taught you?'

'To be happy with nothing,' he replied.

This seems to be a running theme in my work at the Happiness Research Institute, in my books and also when planning things to do with friends and family: how do we decouple wellbeing from wealth? How do we create a good life on a low budget? How do we remove the price tag from happiness?

In happiness research, we often stumble upon the 'hedonic treadmill'. It is the psychological concept that we humans seem to continually raise the bar for what we think we need in order to be happy. That goes for income level, the size of your office or your house, or the title on your business card.

Let me ask you: what would it take to make you feel rich? Well, it probably depends on how much you have now. At least that is what we conclude from the data. People in the US have been asked this question and as you can see from the table on the next page, the more money people are making already, the more they think they need to feel rich.

For instance, would an annual income of $150,000 make you feel rich? Of people who are currently making below $50,000, 50 per cent say yes – and so do 25 per cent of people making between $50,000 and $99,999, but only 7 per cent of people making $100,000 or more. We raise the bar for what we feel we need.

The problem is there is always a higher number. And so, people will always be craving more and more money. The thing is, even if you get to the astronomical number you dreamed of – and perhaps sacrificed other priorities in your life along the way – and finally get to sit there in your Gulfstream G700 private jet, you realize: 'That's it? That's what all the hype was about? I don't feel fulfilled. Darn it, I am still not happy.' Apparently, that hole in your heart was not G700 jet-shaped.

Then you realize that the great philosopher Jim Carrey was right all along when he said: 'I think everybody should get rich and famous and do everything they ever dreamed of, so they can see that it's not the answer.'

The challenge is that our first experience with a paycheque tells us that more money equals more happiness – so we get wired that way. Yes, money and happiness are correlated, because having no money will make you unhappy – and the first money we get we spend on food and housing. But after a certain threshold, additional income doesn't move the needle when it comes to your happiness – not even the dog is happier because of his new coat.

So, while money does impact your happiness, we must not use it as the yardstick of success, nor as our only compass when choosing work.

WOULD YOU FEEL RICH?

	'Yes' from those earning below $50,000	'Yes' from those earning between $50,000 and $99,999	'Yes' from those earning $100,000 or above
Under $15,000	5	0	0
$15,000–$29,999	3	0	0
$30,000–$49,999	5	1	0
$50,000–$74,999	9	3	1
$75,000–$99,999	9	6	1
$100,000–$149,999	19	15	5
$150,000–$199,999	10	16	8
$200,000–$499,999	11	23	25
$500,000–$999,999	10	15	27
$1 million or more	18	19	30

Change the Narrative

The long game here is also that we have to change the narrative of what success looks like. A challenge that a lot of young people are facing is that they feel they can choose to become one of the following three things: a doctor, a lawyer, or a disappointment. They feel a lot of pressure from parents or society or both to choose a profession that provides the illusion of success. Would you rather have a daughter who is an unhappy doctor instead of a happy whatever? Hopefully not. I am sure that a lot of parents in Denmark also want (and to some extent try to influence) their sons and daughters to become doctors and lawyers, but it seems that in this country children are generally encouraged to pursue an education in whatever they are interested in and have a talent for.

I would have been a lousy lawyer – legal documents make me sleepy – and I would have been an unconscious doctor – the sight of blood makes me faint. Fortunately, I enjoyed studying people; why we do what we do and how what we do makes us feel. Good qualities for a happiness researcher, in short.

Back in 2012, I told my dad that I was quitting my job, where I had worked for almost seven years. It was a well-paid stable job as international director for a Danish think tank.

'So, what are you going to do instead?' he asked.

'Well, I am going to study happiness. I want to start a think tank called the Happiness Research Institute.'

There was silence for a second. Then, 'I think that sounds like a great idea.'

Some might have thought that starting a think tank on happiness was not the right thing to do – especially as the world was then still dealing with the consequences of the 2008 financial crisis. But since I was very young, my dad had always reminded me to focus on the satisfaction you get from work, not the paycheque. 'You are going to spend a huge part of your life working – it should be something you enjoy,' he would say.

Being successful should mean feeling good about what you do – and doing good work feels great. Happiness is the ultimate success.

That is why you should seek out work that makes you feel proud, that makes you feel good, work that you are good at – and perhaps it is time to kiss the imposter syndrome goodbye.

£ Happiness

The Real Imposter

In 1978, Pauline Clance and Suzanne Imes, two researchers at Georgia State University, published a paper in the journal *Psychotherapy: Theory, Research and Practice*, which spread like wildfire, because it described a phenomenon that so many people, particularly high-achieving women, had experienced: the 'imposter phenomenon'.

Clance and Imes, who had both experienced the feeling themselves, joined forces, spent five years talking to more than 150 successful women and developed the idea of the imposter phenomenon, describing it as 'an internal experience of intellectual phoniness', living in perpetual fear that 'some significant person will discover that they are indeed intellectual impostors'.

The concept gained traction and an Imposter Phenomenon Scale was developed for researchers to apply in studies. But when social media emerged, the concept, now dubbed imposter syndrome, exploded. At the time of writing, the search term 'imposter syndrome' yields 5.7 million hits on Google and people like former First Lady and international bestselling author Michelle Obama, Supreme Court Justice Sonia Sotomayor, movie star Charlize Theron, business executive Sheryl Sandberg and former IMF head Christine Lagarde have all claimed to have experienced it.

Evidently, as Clance and Imes argued in their original paper, success is not a cure. What Clance later found, working with clients, was that group therapy worked well. Listening to *other* women – *successful* women – talking about having the same feelings, of feeling like imposters, worked. It was easier to believe that these other women were not imposters – so maybe you're not either.

However, four decades after the original article was published, another duo of researchers argued that we have been looking at the imposter phenomenon all wrong. It is not *you* that has a flaw we need to fix, it is *the system* that is rotten.

In 2021, Ruchika Tulshyan and Jodi-Ann Burey published an article in *Harvard Business Review* that became one of the most widely shared articles in the history of the magazine. It was called 'Stop Telling Women They Have Imposter Syndrome'.

Tulshyan and Burey argued that the term imposter syndrome implies that it is you who is wrong, turning the problem into an individual pathology, and removes the focus on the systemic inequality facing women, especially women of colour. There are real obstacles to contend with, such as biases in hiring, promotion, leadership and compensation – or as Tulshyan and Burey put it: 'Imposter syndrome directs our view toward fixing women at work instead of fixing the places where women work.'

So, ironically, perhaps the imposter syndrome was the imposter, with really high levels of self-esteem. And in fact, when you look at fixing the system, it starts to become clear who benefits from us feeling like imposters. According to an article in the *New Yorker*, 'Capitalism needs us *all* to feel like impostors, because feeling like an impostor ensures we'll strive for endless progress: work harder, make more money, try to be better than our former selves and the people around us.' The biggest threat to capitalism is us feeling happy. Think about it: if everyone was happy with what they had, companies wouldn't be able to sell anything and we wouldn't need to push ourselves at work for the next pay rise, the bigger car or the fancy holiday. Remember that TV show about the advertising industry in the 1960s. The main character summed it up quite nicely: 'Advertising is based on one thing:

happiness. And you know what happiness is? Happiness is the smell of a new car. It's freedom from fear. It's a billboard on the side of the road that screams reassurance that whatever you're doing, it's okay. You are okay.'

But you are already better than okay. You should not feel like a fraud, you should feel good about the work that you do, because your self-esteem matters for your happiness at work.

The Importance of Self-Esteem

At the Happiness Research Institute, we have run a lot of studies that measure, track and analyse happiness levels among employees, and one of the areas we focus on as an indicator of happiness is self-esteem. We often use Rosenberg's Self-Esteem Scale and ask questions like, on a scale of 1 to 10, to what extent do you agree with the statement that:

'I feel I have a number of good qualities.'

'I feel I do not have much to be proud of.'

'I certainly feel useless at times.'

We can see in the data that self-esteem explains differences in happiness at work and happiness in general. What we also find is that men usually report higher levels of self-esteem, which I guess supports the mantra: 'May we all have the self-confidence of a mediocre white man.'

One of the studies we conducted, run in a company of 200 employees, showed us that people with high self-esteem were more likely to agree with the following statements:

'I feel that I am good at my job.'

'I feel supported by my manager.'

'I know what is expected of me at work.'

While I was at university, I had a job in a café in the Botanical Gardens in Copenhagen. On sunny days, hordes of people would come to us in urgent need of ice cream, beer and coffee – and my colleague Chila and I would just crush it. We worked side by side for years; we knew the details of every task and could find ways to optimize every job in the café. Chila would use one hand to hold the beer glass under the tap, her other hand to pass me the whipped cream for the hot chocolate, while opening the fridge with her foot and cracking a joke to a customer . . . working was a game that looked like a mix between gymnastics, ballet and improv theatre.

We had no skin in the game when it came to the turnover of the café, but we loved it when we felt we had set a new record, giving guests super-efficient and friendly service. One day, Kim and Ricardo, who owned the café, stood in line, waiting their turn, just to let us know how happy and proud they were that we were working there. We were great, and that job was great for my self-esteem. I felt very competent. A cappuccino, you say – let me get that for you, super-quick with perfect foam. It was easy to see when I had done a good job and that my skills were getting better and better.

So, if you're lacking in self-esteem at work and you're not sure why or what you can do about it, think about how much you agree with the statements on the left and how you can improve that score. Feeling that you're good at what you do is particularly important. When we explore why some Danes report more happiness at work than others, a sense of mastery is one of the top factors.

Mastery is all about feeling you can handle the tasks and situations you encounter in life. At work, mastery means feeling good at what you are paid to do, it means feeling competent to handle the tasks you're asked to complete, and that is vital to achieving happiness at work. Handling tasks, perhaps even increasingly difficult tasks, and developing your skill set to tackle those challenges are surely going to

drive your wellbeing at work, and that is what success should feel like. Not driving a fancy car – but doing difficult stuff.

As Steve Jobs has been credited with saying: 'Your work is going to fill a large part of your life, and the only way to be truly satisfied is to do what you believe is great work. And the only way to do great work is to love what you do. If you haven't found it yet, keep looking. Don't settle. As with all matters of the heart, you'll know when you find it.'

HAPPINESS TIP: GAMIFY WORK

When we get the balance right between the level of difficulty of the task and the level of competence to solve it, we may experience 'flow'. The term 'flow' is often discussed in relation to positive psychology techniques and was first introduced by Mihaly Csikszentmihalyi, a professor of psychology at the University of Chicago. Flow is when you are so absorbed in the task at hand that you lose track of time and that little nagging voice in your head is silent for once. It is a pleasant state to be in, and Csikszentmihalyi found that artists and athletes especially would experience flow.

'You see this ball?'

'Yes.'

'Well, I want you to put it in a small hole.'

'Any small hole?'

'No, a specific small hole. It is 400 metres in that direction. I've put a flag next to it so you can see it.'

'Ah yes. Okay, give me the ball and I'll put it in.'

'No, you can't touch it. You have to hit it over there with a club.'

'What?'

'A club. You swing it like this, see?'

'But that's going to go wrong and the ball is going to land in the water or that pile of sand over there.'

'Most likely, yes. But here is the best part. You have to get that ball in the hole with the club with the least number of strokes.'

'Oh, my lord – give me the club.'

'No.'

'No? But you just told me to put the ball in the hole.'

'Well, if you pay me a hundred pounds, you get to put the small ball in the hole.'

'Okay, please take my money.'

When it comes to happiness at work, we might make things more enjoyable by telling ourselves that it is a game. Basically, by Tom Sawyering yourself. Tricking yourself into having fun painting the fence. Sorry. Here is an apple.

Instead of getting the small ball in the small hole in the fewest strokes possible – how many things can you cross out on your to-do list in two hours? After that, rest and repeat. Think about it like an athlete. How many points can you score in those two hours or thirty minutes? Or how fast can you make the perfect cappuccino?

HAPPINESS TIP: BREAK IT DOWN

Whenever I have a big, complicated work task I need to complete, I break it down into a long list of smaller tasks, which makes the bigger task more enjoyable, because I can see that I am slowly checking off the small tasks, one by one. This is how video games are built, and I know the effect they have on me. I've spent a large portion of my life on games like *Rick Dangerous*, *Bubble Bobble*, *Super Mario Bros.* (yes, I was a kid in the 80s) – and I cannot have *Hay Day* anywhere near me because it is essentially like heroin to me. Each level in the game leads to the next.

The Pomodoro Technique might be especially useful, if you have a long project or a lot of open-ended work that can take weeks or months to finish. Like writing a research proposal or studying for an exam, for instance.

1. Write a to-do list and use a timer.

2. Set the timer for 25 minutes and focus on a single task for that period.

3. When the timer rings, record what you have done in that session and perhaps cross one item off the to-do list.

4. Take a 5-minute break.

5. After four sessions, take a 15–30-minute break.

If you want to write a book, shrink the task down to an unintimidating first step, like sitting and writing for two minutes. If this is too hard, sit down and write the first sentence of a chapter. One of my favourite opening lines of a book is: 'Barrabás came to us by sea, the child Clara wrote in her delicate calligraphy.' It is fourteen words. You can do this!

Sometimes great things have small beginnings, and doing something small can make it easier to take on something big.

We also tend to overestimate what we can do in a day and underestimate what we can do in a year – or have done in the past year. I always enjoy looking back on the past twelve months and listing all that I have achieved. We tend to focus on the mountain in front of us and forget how far we have actually come.

'We' Over 'Me'

A few years ago, on a visit to Riga, I saw a huge luxury car in the street. It had a personalized licence plate: 'SUCCESS'. But where success may be enthusiastically flaunted in Latvia and other countries, humility is the bigger virtue in Denmark.

In Copenhagen, that car would have been keyed within twenty-four hours. Success is not something you flaunt. It is something you don't really talk about, let alone put on a licence plate. That is because of the Law of Jante – or *'Janteloven'* in both Danish and Norwegian, *'Jantelagen'* in Swedish, *'Jante laki'* in Finnish and *'Jantelögin'* in Icelandic – which illustrates a social code specific to the Nordic region. It emphasizes collective accomplishments and looks down on focusing on individual achievements.

The 'law' originates from the 1933 novel *A Fugitive Crosses His Tracks* by Danish-Norwegian author Aksel Sandemose. Its message can be boiled down to 'you're no better than us'.

THE LAW OF JANTE

1. You're not to think *you* are anything special.

2. You're not to think *you* are as good as *we* are.

3. You're not to think *you* are smarter than *we* are.

4. You're not to convince yourself that *you* are better than *we* are.

5. You're not to think *you* know more than *we* do.

6. You're not to think *you* are more important than *we* are.

7. You're not to think *you* are good at anything.

8. You're not to laugh at *us*.

9. You're not to think anyone cares about *you*.

10. You're not to think *you* can teach *us* anything.

Some of these lines feel a bit harsh and at odds with other lessons in this book, but a general aversion to trumpeting individual success or excellence continues to be prevalent across Scandinavian cultures. It is why the Danish beer Carlsberg claims to be 'probably the best beer in the world' and not simply 'the best beer in the world'. *Janteloven* promotes a culture where successful people can be criticized if they pretend to be better than their peers. You may know this as 'tall-poppy syndrome' in English.

The Law of Jante definitely has some negative implications for the Nordic societies and the wellbeing of Scandinavia as a whole, such as putting a cap on how you might celebrate something you have accomplished – but I think its upside is that success is often articulated as a shared accomplishment.

It is also why Danes in the workplace are more likely to talk about success stories in terms of 'we'. We did this. The team accomplished that. And to use 'I' when it comes to failures and shortfalls.

And that might be the lesson from Denmark. Shower your team and co-workers with praise of their success. In my experience, happiness, self-esteem, success and perfume all have this shared trait: you can't pour it on someone without getting some on yourself.

HAPPINESS TIP: EMPLOYEE OF THE MONTH WITH A TWIST

―――――――――――――――

A few years ago, one of the speakers at a workshop at the Happiness Research Institute was a head nurse from Rigshospitalet, the main hospital in Copenhagen. On his ward they had had to deal with difficulties in communication between some of the nurses. 'The challenge is,' he said, 'our job sometimes involves checking that our co-workers have done things right. Making sure a patient has received the right dose of medicine and so on. So, a lot of people felt they were being criticized by their colleagues.'

The somewhat negative climate meant that the ward was dealing with a high level of sick days being taken. So, they came up with an innovative take on the old 'employee of the month' concept. Imagine that you and I are nurses on this ward, and on our latest shift together, I saved a patient's life. At the next morning's team meeting, you tell everybody – and our boss – what an amazing job I did yesterday. Yay me!

What happens next is that *you* are made employee of the month this month because you told everyone about my finest hour. Because we want to cultivate a culture where we are each other's ambassadors, where we are encouraged to spread the success stories of our colleagues. This little tweak changed the atmosphere on the ward and led to a significant drop in sick days.

The Chicken and the Egg

People might see what looks like a successful person and think, 'Well, they look happy.' But what if we have got the order wrong? What if happiness leads to success?

Earlier, I mentioned the British Telecom study that showed that happier workers are more productive. Remember that great conversation you had with your boss?

Well, that study is not alone. More than ten years ago now, Andrew Oswald, Eugenio Proto and Daniel Sgroi from the Economics Faculty at the University of Warwick conducted four controlled experiments involving 700 participants, and they found that happiness at work can increase productivity by 12 per cent. Similarly, 'The Job Satisfaction-Productivity Nexus: A Study Using Matched Survey and Register Data' looked at Finnish manufacturing companies over a five-year period and found that an increase in employee satisfaction led to a productivity increase of 6.6 per cent.

However, one of the most comprehensive studies of the link between wellbeing and productivity was conducted by Sonja Lyubomirsky, Laura King and Ed Diener, who are professors of psychology at UCLA, the University of Missouri and the University of Illinois respectively. They conducted a meta study looking at 225 pieces of academic research into the link between happiness at work and success. They found that there is strong evidence for a causal link from happiness leading to a successful company. Or as Shawn Anchor, Harvard University researcher and author of *The Happiness Advantage*, says: 'Happiness is perhaps the most overlooked reason for success.'

And the evidence continues to stack up – rather than seeking happiness from success and money, happiness should come first. At least that is what Professor Andrew Oswald and Dr Jan-Emmanuel De Neve from the Oxford Wellbeing Research Centre found.

Using data from Add Health – a large sample of representative individuals in the US who have been bombarded with questions (including questions around wellbeing and income over a long period of time) – they found that people's happiness levels in their teenage years and early twenties predicted their income levels in their late twenties and early thirties.

Happier people seem more likely to get a degree, find a job and be promoted. So, if you are one point happier on a five-point scale at the age of twenty-two, you are going to make $2,000 a year more by the time you are twenty-nine. The results of the study are robust and include controls for variables such as education, IQ, physical health, height, self-esteem and later happiness. Since the data includes thousands of siblings, the study can also discount the effect of parents. The happier sibling is going to make more money later on.

So maybe it is time to use happiness as the new measure of success. After all, as Aristotle put it more than 2,000 years ago: happiness is the ultimate aim of human existence.

HAPPINESS TIP: SIGN YOUR NAME ACROSS YOUR WORK

We all want to put our stamp on the world. Leave a mark. Sign our name on what we've created.

I was recently in Saint-Vincent-de-Paul, about 20 kilometres north-east of Bordeaux, for the inauguration of the Maroquinerie de Guyenne, an artisan leather workshop where Hermès employ around 300 people. I was moderating a round-table discussion about happiness at work for the company and they had invited me to take a closer look at how their production worked. Hermès is no stranger to happiness at work. The company ranks first out of the 500 best employers in France according to the French magazine *Capital*, but perhaps a stronger testimony is that the average length of service at Hermès is nine years. Over a third of the workforce has been there for more than ten years and 12 per cent of employees have been there twenty years or longer.

Karl Marx believed that work, at its best, is what makes us human. It allows us to live, be creative and flourish. He hated how capitalism alienated workers from each other and from the product of their labour. However, 140 years after his death, there *are* companies going in the opposite direction and allowing the workers to follow the fruit of their labour from start to finish, and even put their name on it. Maybe Marx would not have expected to find his ideas being put into practice in a company like Hermès.

'I am not a single link in a chain,' one Hermès artisan says. 'I master the job from the start to the end. We are taught a craft, not a series of tasks. And in the end, I put my signature on the bag. We feel personally responsible for the work that we do. These days, that is a wonderful opportunity.' Stitching the way people did 400 years ago and completing entire bags by themselves, these artisans have to master many different tools and skills. (Yes, I do realize the bags are really expensive, but a similar practice is implemented by Son of a Tailor, a t-shirt company that produces made-to-measure t-shirts, where the seamstresses also put their name on the shirts after creating them from start to finish.)

Now, imagine the difference in terms of satisfaction between creating an entire bag or a shirt, and getting to put your name on it, compared to washing the wire that eventually gets turned into pins at the pin factory. Yes, I know Adam Smith would argue about productivity and the cost of the pins – but we are talking about the impact on happiness here, Adam.

Great and simple ways to make your mark on your work clearly count for a lot. While we can't all put our names on products we have created, I believe the lesson here is value in terms of workers' satisfaction. If we can find a way to connect employees to the product of their labour, we should take it. And if we can't put our name on the product, maybe there is still a way to put our stamp on it somehow. A hidden Easter egg somewhere in the software code, or mentioning Winnie the Pooh in all of your books – or spelling out WIKING using the first letter in each of the paragraphs in this Tip, for instance . . .

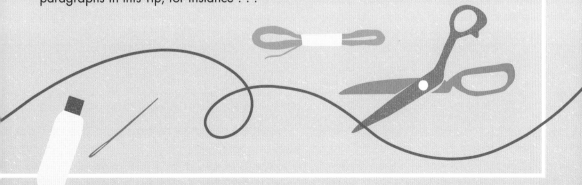

HAPPYWORK

❏ I'm sorry, but it is time to write your own obituary. I know this is a bit of a morbid exercise, but writing an obituary for yourself is a useful way to think about your life in general. It is a way to recognize where you are and where you are headed – and whether you should change course a bit. It may also help you with setting new or better goals for what a successful life means to you. Start by answering questions like: What did I spend my time doing? What were the relationships that I built? How did I make the world a better place? What did I say yes to in life? How will people remember me?

❏ Mitigate the one-more-million syndrome. If you are already making a decent income, challenge the belief that how happy you feel will be radically different with a different number in your bank balance.

❏ Consider which jobs, tasks, hobbies and activities give you flow and which make you feel proud and accomplished, and how you can incorporate them more into your life, in or out of work.

❏ Try applying the Pomodoro Technique to a large complex task you have before you, either at work or at home. Break it down into smaller manageable tasks, give yourself 25 minutes to focus on just one of them, then take a 5-minute break and repeat.

❏ Go for value instead of success. Maybe it is my Nordic upbringing that has made me take Albert Einstein's advice – 'Try not to become a man of success. Rather become a man of value' – to heart, but I find that value is a much better compass for your career. Whereas success comes with an external view, value starts with you. It means understanding what you are good at and what you can add to a team, an organization or the world.

CHAPTER

7

—

THE FUTURE
OF WELLBEING
AT WORK

The future of wellbeing at work is a topic of growing importance, as technology continues to advance and work becomes more demanding. The rise of remote work, the gig economy and the mental and physical health challenges caused by the COVID-19 pandemic have all contributed to the need for better workplace wellbeing programmes.

One trend that is likely to continue in the future is the integration of technology into wellbeing programmes. Wearable devices and mobile apps can track physical activity and sleep patterns, while virtual reality and telehealth services can provide mental health support remotely. These tools can provide employees with real-time feedback on their wellbeing and allow managers to identify potential issues early on.

. . . so, that introduction was written by artificial intelligence. I think it is quite amusing how technology is mentioned in the very first sentence, that wellbeing at work is growing in importance as technology advances. Calm down, Willy Loman, no need to get all salesy on us in your opening line – and hold the free set of steak knives.

Wellbeing at work is growing in importance because we recognize that we need to redesign the way we work to add to our wellbeing, instead of undermining it. That said, our AI colleague may be right: I do see technology playing an increasing role in tracking our wellbeing at work. Already there is an app available that can read your current emotional state by analysing your face. Are you angry, anxious or happy? This emotional recognition software is a first-generation technology, still in its early stages. If I show my teeth, the software thinks I am smiling and suggests that I am happy. But as we all know, we can smile without being happy.

'Hey, Lester, got a minute?'

'For you, Brad, I got five.'

If this reference is lost on you – you need to watch *American Beauty*. No time for questions, just go watch it when you are done with this chapter . . .

But ten years down the line, with a third-generation technology, your phone will have access to the tone of your voice, your online behaviour, how active you are during the day, and it will know where you are and with whom. It will likely know whether you are depressed before even your friends and family do.

Siri: 'Meik, I noticed that you been feeling down lately. You have an opening in your calendar on Tuesday – should I set up an appointment with your therapist? She has availability.'

AI is going to revolutionize work in certain fields. The global corporation PwC (PricewaterhouseCoopers) predicts that 3 per cent of jobs are already at risk from AI. By the mid-2030s, this share will jump to 30 per cent, and 44 per cent among workers with low education. So perhaps it is time to look more closely at another development that could revolutionize how we think about work.

Universal Basic Income

In 2017, Finland began a two-year experiment. They wondered what would happen if people were paid a basic income without anything being demanded of them in return. No need to apply for jobs, no need for meetings with a job agency, no excuses needed for not working.

The idea was not new. Cities like Barcelona in Spain, Stockton in the US, Maricá in Brazil and the province of Gyeonggi in South Korea have all been experimenting with universal basic income. But this was the first time a full country brought the idea to life.

The Finnish government randomly picked 2,000 people who were unemployed at the time. For the next two years they automatically received a cash payment of €560 each month, plus a housing allowance which they all qualified for of €330 – a total of €890 per month.

This is not a lobster-and-caviar-level budget. The average employed Finn has a disposable monthly income of €2,400, while Finnish students have about €1,000. Nevertheless, the allowance would be enough to get by, living frugally, without having to work.

The 2,000 randomly selected people were the trial group and all other unemployed people, who continued to receive their standard benefits, were the control group.

The hope was that, without the nuisance of having to deal with bureaucracy, the people on universal basic income would be more likely to get a job or start their own business. And the experiment showed that that actually happened – the people in the trial group were more likely to be employed than those in the control group – although the effect was only small.

The biggest effect was actually found in wellbeing, where a significant boost was detected. When the experiment finished, the people with universal basic income reported an average happiness of 7.3 on a scale from 0 to 10, compared with 6.8 in the control group. Half a point may not seem like a big difference, but the life satisfaction needle is notoriously hard to move. The average effect on life satisfaction from getting married is around half a point. In addition, people with universal basic income experienced better health and lower levels of stress, sadness, depression and loneliness compared to people in the control group.

My hope is that we will see more governments be brave enough to conduct similar experiments, allowing people to venture into entrepreneurship or artistic endeavours with a more tight-knit safety net underneath them. At the Happiness Museum in Copenhagen, we like to ask people what law they would pass if they were the Minister of Happiness in their country. 'Everybody should get a Corgi,' one wrote. 'Make owning a bike mandatory,' wrote another. I second those proposals, but interestingly, the three most frequently proposed ideas for laws that people would pass are universal health care, a four-day working week and universal basic income.

And besides universal basic income and technological advances, there is another development that won't cost a thing and will help us create better workplaces: an acceptance of the f-word in business.

The F-Word in Business

The f-word is different in the corporate world: feelings. Companies usually don't talk about feelings or emotions or happiness. However, in the decade I've been working in happiness research, I've noticed that a shift is happening.

For instance, I recently conducted a workshop for an international company's executive group, who had asked me to spend a day with them focusing on happiness research and what they could learn from it. We started out with a show-and-tell session, where everybody had brought an object, or a picture of an object, that was a symbol of happiness for them. I find this is a lovely way to kick off such a day as it allows us to talk very specifically about what happiness is and it is also a great way to get to know people.

One had brought a picture of her daughters, one had brought a boomerang, one had brought a dog collar . . . the group of twelve people had all brought different things – but they had also brought heartwarming stories of happiness, love, loss, joy and eating crayfish on a rooftop. All of the stories were moving – and most of the group started crying as they told or heard them. I even teared up and I did not know these people. I am not crying – you're crying! Not exactly how you would expect a workshop on happiness to start. But these were tears of joy and it really brought the group together and made sure they will remember that workshop years from now. That would not have happened ten years ago.

Talking about emotions at work has become more common – and tracking them as well. At the Happiness Research Institute, we have worked with several companies to help them measure the wellbeing of their employees by taking more of an interest in their feelings as well as their output.

Tracking respondents over time helps both us and the company understand how their employees' wellbeing is evolving, but you have to be asking the right questions. Perhaps half of your workforce feel the same, 10 per cent are less happy and 40 per cent of the employees are happier than a year ago. This might seem like a good result, but if you are only measuring the average job satisfaction or engagement in your organization, an increase in that average might just mean that the unhappy ones left and that you hired a happy bunch (whose wellbeing might be undermined in the coming year).

One company we were working with recognized from asking more feeling-focused questions that a lot of people were experiencing loneliness, and so we conducted a series of workshops on the topic. Here we discovered that when people were hired just out of university, they would get a comprehensive onboarding programme, including classes and social activities with the other recent graduates who had just started at the company. They would also be assigned a buddy to function as their informal mentor, to show them the ropes. In contrast, if you were hired in a more senior role, you were more or less shown to your desk with a simple 'welcome on board'. Because of the nature of the business, people were only in the office one day a week and on the road the rest of the time – and thus it took longer to build relationships at the office. One person described how their first three months at the company had been the loneliest time of their life. Thereafter, the company changed the onboarding procedure for senior staff, making it a less lonely experience.

The point is that no matter what you do, you are working with people, not employees. We feel stressed and lonely and a whole array of different emotions at work, both positive and negative. For the Happiness Research Institute, one of the key challenges has been deciding where to draw the line in terms of what we can ask people. 'How satisfied are you with work?' seems like a valid and legitimate question to ask – but how about 'How often do you feel there are people who really understand you? Often, some of the time, hardly ever or never?' Or 'Would you agree with the following statement: "I do not have much to be proud of"?'

Questions like these, from the UCLA Loneliness Scale and Rosenberg's Self-Esteem Scale, explain why some people are more happy or less happy at work – and in fact with life in general. From a scientific point of view, it makes sense to include them, but in practice a lot of companies are hesitant to do so because they believe these topics are too personal to bring up in a work survey. But things are changing.

We are increasingly acknowledging that our work spills over into the other parts of our lives, and vice versa. If I am stressed at work, that will influence my life with my family and friends. Loneliness, self-esteem, stress and joy spill over from one domain to the other, which is why I believe the idea of 'work–life balance' to be a myth. If you feel unhappy at work, that is going to influence your overall happiness. If you feel lonely at work, that is going to influence your wellbeing – at work and at home.

What Do You Offer in Terms of Happiness?

Nobody wants to spend a third of their waking hours around miserable people doing miserable things for miserable reasons. We all want to do work that we enjoy. But where to find it? Working this out was tricky in the past; perhaps you knew somebody working at the company you were considering applying to and could ask if they enjoyed their work, but often you didn't have that option. The good news is that more and more job-search sites are collecting data on happiness at work, and publishing it, to help jobseekers take it into account.

Previously, we could choose between Job A, which paid £30,000, and Job B, which paid £29,000; the job titles and descriptions were the same, and the distance from your home for each job was the same. You would go with Job A, right? But what if 100 previous and current employees rated their happiness level at Job A as 3.1 out of 5, whereas the score was 4.3 out of 5 at Job B? Wouldn't you go with Job B?

The Italian astronomer Galileo Galilei once said, 'Measure the measurable – and make the unmeasurable measurable.' That is what we strive for as happiness researchers, to quantify something as subjective and complex as happiness.

Salary is so easy to measure – and has therefore perhaps had too much influence when we contemplate where to work. But now we can compare happiness levels too. And no, just because a lot of former and current employees experience a happiness level of 4.3 at Company B that doesn't mean that you will too, and just because people working for Company A experience work happiness levels of 3.1 that does not mean that you will too. But don't you want to play the odds?

To take an example, Ryanair scores 3.1 and Southwest Airlines scores 4.3 on the job site indeed.com. The reviews include a written report as well as a score, and some of the titles say it all: 'Great pay and benefits – awful everything else.' Of course, we can't all just pick the job with the highest level of work happiness. Some people might need the higher pay to make ends meet. But I believe it is useful and valuable for many people to take into consideration how well a potential employer delivers wellbeing to its employees. Adding this into the equation could make a huge difference to your overall happiness.

Take on the Role of
Chief Happiness Officer

Earlier I mentioned that many companies like Google have added Chief Happiness Officers to their staff. This is great but, just like green-washing, where companies pretend to be more eco-friendly than they really are, beware of happy-washing. There is a difference between saying you want to make your employees happier and actually doing it. Unfortunately, I have seen companies make bold statements about happiness but shy away from delivering the key components of a happiness policy.

But Chief Happiness Officer does not have to be an official role. We all have a responsibility for colleagues' wellbeing at work – and, most importantly, our own. Consider how far you can go to find out about the happiness levels in your workplace. Can you ask your employees or your co-workers how satisfied they are with life? What about how lonely they feel? Different cultures will have different boundaries for what should be off limits and what is too personal, and people should always have the option not to answer these kinds of questions. The key thing is to try to shift the focus onto happiness first, as productivity is guaranteed to follow.

Yes, companies have a responsibility for your wellbeing at work, but so do you. In this book, I've tried to shed light on some of the things you can do to improve how you feel about work, like job crafting, but also how to empower yourself financially to be able to quit a crappy job or escape a toxic boss.

Beyond Paid Work

I have worked as a cleaner, a baker, a dad, a journalist, a barista, a home maker and a groundskeeper.

I've worked in a planetarium, a ministry of foreign affairs, a botanical garden, in a bookstore selling Spanish and French books and in a movie theatre – my favourite bit there was seeing the reaction when the audience watching *Seven* got to the bit where it turned out the guy they thought was dead was not dead (no, no spoiler alert, this movie is from 1995 – if you haven't watched it by now you never will).

I've started a magazine about photography, a think tank on happiness and a novel that will never be finished. I've sold Christmas trees and ice cream. My favourite part of *that* role was having a customer point towards the stracciatella, saying that they would like a scoop of the one they couldn't pronounce. I then offered them banana.

I've worked in data entry – literally changing 2s to 3s (this was pre-Y2K stuff. If you are too young to know what Y2K is, good for you), and organized conferences (through that job, I learned that one particular former UN secretary-general requires a 4/5ths'-full glass of water within reach at all times. That is one thirsty ego . . .)

In undertaking these various different roles, I have learned the recipe for 150-kilo batches of cinnamon yumminess, I can tell the difference between a red spruce and a Norway spruce, I know how to find the star Arcturus using the Big Dipper, and I can even give you a good recipe for happiness (it is very close to the cinnamon yumminess one, by the way).

Work is not just about the paycheque. With every job, we pick up things that bring value to our lives: skills, friends, anecdotes. Some of my best friends today are from the movie gang I worked with at the cinema. I still use the negotiation skills I picked up selling Christmas trees for seven years, and I still talk about the time I was in a Ferrari Formula 1 car driven by Charles Leclerc, travelling at 300 kilometres per hour in Monza, Italy (one of the side benefits of being a happiness researcher).

No job is perfect, and we all have bad days at work and tasks that are less fulfilling and fun. Not even Danes experience work Valhalla – where we fight (the old Norse idea of fun) all day and feast all night. But work is part of life. An important part. And it should be a largely enjoyable part – if we design it right. If we build or aim to work for organizations that trust their employees. Organizations that provide them with a liveable salary, as well as a sense of purpose and accomplishment. Organizations that enable their people to connect and flourish.

But some of us may source those ingredients in different places. We may get our sense of purpose from raising our kids, and our sense of accomplishment from *finally* putting up that bookshelf. In the same way, we may use our life beyond the nine-to-five to give us opportunities to counter what might at times feel like a soul-sucking job. Cycling to work and cooking our food at home are just some of the ways we can reduce our spending in order to build our Freedom Fund, which can enable us to perhaps spend less time at work – or to completely pull the plug on it one day.

My hope is also that we will widen our definition of work. 'Work' doesn't only mean paid work. It is also nurturing a veg patch at home for you and your family, or working on creating a better social fabric in your neighbourhood – or writing that sci-fi rom-com novel. Paid work is essential to make a living but it does not make a life.

I believe that to be happier at work we must also design our lives in a different way. We should live closer to work or adjust our commute so that we can walk or bike at least some of the way there, reduce our spending so we can save for an FU fund and spend time with family and friends on projects that give us a sense of connection, combined with a sense of accomplishment.

Earlier this year, I was talking with Camelot (The National Lottery in the UK) about their big-ticket winners: those who had won a million pounds or more, the people with the big cheques you see in the papers. We were discussing how differences in spending patterns would impact their happiness. One of their winners, a guy who had been working night shifts at the local dog-food company, woke up one day as a millionaire. He quit his job, but he did not quit working altogether. He bought a ride-on lawnmower and started a business mowing people's lawns. After all those years working in the factory at night and sleeping during the day, he enjoyed sitting on his tractor in the sunshine. Having money didn't mean he wanted to do nothing all day – it wasn't the solution to happiness, it just gave him more freedom. But feeling more free is within our power without winning the lottery.

Remember the people I mentioned earlier, who live frugally and invest the bulk of their take-home pay with the plan of living off the dividends and retiring early, some even at the age of thirty? Almost none of them retire in the traditional sense. None, or very few of them, spend the rest of their lives on a beach somewhere sipping piña coladas. They continue to work. The difference is that now they work when they want to and, most importantly, they only take on work they enjoy, since they don't need the income any more.

I think that, as humans, we are wired to work. We enjoy achieving things. Personally, I feel happier and more satisfied with myself and my life when I've had a day when I have been productive, as opposed to when I have done nothing.

This continues after our paid-work careers have ended. Many retirees struggle with their new lives. How to fill their days, where to find purpose, structure and people to connect with. So, even though retirement might be years or decades away, it is worth considering what you might do with that time. I personally plan to finish that crime novel I've been working on for twenty years now (it is a mix between *Borgen* and *The Killing*). And I want to plant a large fruit orchard on some land and make jams and brew cider. Oh, and I want to build a big wooden catapult.

But until I reach that point, I will continue to spread knowledge about how we can improve the quality of our lives, including how we can work like the happiest people in the world. By looking for purpose and freedom, by trusting and connecting with others, by embracing the work–life blend, and by reframing success.

Perhaps it was best said by Bessie Anderson Stanley, an American writer who wrote the poem 'What Is Success?': 'He has achieved success who has lived well, laughed often, and loved much; [. . .] who has left the world better than he found it whether by an improved poppy, a perfect poem or a rescued soul; who has never lacked appreciation of Earth's beauty or failed to express it . . .'

HAPPYWORK

❑ Start tracking your wellbeing at work. Don't wait for the company to put surveys in place – just keep a weekly score of how much you enjoyed work that week. For bonus points, you may write a line or two that justifies the score. That will help you to understand what happens during good or bad weeks.

❑ If you are unhappy with your current role, explore job sites like indeed.com that publish happiness scores from current and former employees. This may help you to get a sense of which companies in your field deliver the most happiness to their staff.

❑ Adopt a wider definition of work than just paid work. If your ordinary job can provide you with a sense of purpose, great. But if that is not the case, consider other areas in life where you can harvest meaning – could it be through volunteer work, raising kids or building a better and more trusting neighbourhood?

❑ Have a plan for what to do after you quit your job or retire. You may be retiring from something – but it is important to have something to retire to as well.

Acknowledgements

———

At the Happiness Research Institute I've had the privilege to work alongside these awesome, smart, fun people with their hearts in the right place:

Kjartan, Xavier, Anne-Sofie, Danielle, Maria R, Rannvá, Gabe, Cindie, Kirsten, Christina, Teis, Marie Louise, Michael M, Marie L, Lisa, Michael B, Johan, Felicia, Maria H, Marie H, Lydia, Anne, Alejandro, Mads, Micah, Alexander, Rebecca, Isabella, Vanessa, Jacob, Emilie, Onor, Eric, Sarah, Peter, Ina, Lucija, Olga, Søren, Camilla, Anna and Helene.

Thank you for working on happiness and for bringing happiness to work.

Picture Credits

pp. 9, 16, 19, 44, 54, 107, 149, 202, 219, 223 © Stocksy

pp. 23, 47, 60, 69, 74, 81, 87, 94, 98, 103, 112, 115, 118, 129, 133, 142, 154, 158, 161, 173, 188, 206, 209 © Getty Images

pp. 31, 34, 101, 177 © Alamy

pp. 43, 51, 67, 73, 155 © Shutterstock

pp. 104, 166, 182, 213 © Unsplash